THE GILL HISTORY OF IRELAND

General Editors: JAMES LYDON, PH.D.
MARGARET MACCURTAIN, PH.D.

Other titles in the series

TUDOR
and STUART
IRELAND

Margaret MacCurtain

GILL AND MACMILLAN

Published in Ireland by
Gill and Macmillan Ltd
Goldenbridge
Dublin 8
with associated companies in
Auckland, Dallas, Delhi, Hong Kong,
Johannesburg, Lagos, London, Manzini,
Melbourne, Nairobi, New York, Singapore,
Tokyo, Washington
© Margaret MacCurtain, 1972
Cover design by Cor Klaasen
7171 0564 4
Print origination in Ireland by
Smurfit Print and Packaging Ltd, Dublin
Printed in Hong Kong

Contents

Foreword

Preface

Foreword

THE study of Irish history has changed greatly in recent decades as more evidence becomes available and new insights are provided by the growing number of historians. It is natural, too, that with each generation new questions should be asked about our past. The time has come for a new large-scale history. It is the aim of the Gill History of Ireland to provide this. This series of studies of Irish history, each written by a specialist, is arranged chronologically. But each volume is intended to stand on its own and no attempt has been made to present a uniform history. Diversity of analysis and interpretation is the aim; a group of young historians have tried to express the view of their generation on our past. It is the hope of the editors that the series will help the reader to appreciate in a new way the rich heritage of Ireland's history.

JAMES LYDON, PH.D.
MARGARET MACCURTAIN, PH.D.

Preface

AT the beginning of the sixteenth century Ireland and
Scotland were remote from the centre of Tudor monarchy.
Scotland possessed a separate king and the Scottish Border
was the division between two separate kingdoms. Ireland
was an island to the west of Britain, and though conquered
in the name of Henry II of England centuries earlier it had,
for practical purposes, escaped subjugation. By the end of
the Tudor century both countries were to be drawn into
closer association with the English Crown, one by succession to the throne, the other by conquest. Scotland's story
does not concern us in this volume except in so far as it
impinges on the history of Ireland. The Tudor conquest of
Ireland and the changes it accomplished in the government,
politics, social and economic life of Ireland form the
subject-matter of this book. It was a conquest which took a
further century of war, plantation and administrative
planning to accomplish. By the end of the seventeenth
century Ireland had been effectively reduced to colonial
status and her social and economic life reflected that
condition.

No special study of these important centuries in their
colonial setting has appeared since the early decades of the
present century. This study is offered as a modest contribution to the understanding of an important aspect of
Irish history and it reflects the interest of the author in the
effect of the plantations upon land and agriculture in
Ireland. Wherever possible, primary sources have been

consulted but – more important to the student – constant reference is made throughout to the many scholarly and specialised studies of problems in sixteenth and seventeenth-century Irish history which have appeared over the last half-century.

The reader may recognise in the following pages the unseen influence of Professor R. D. Edwards for many years teacher, friend and senior colleague of the author. My thanks are offered to Professor J. Lydon, co-editor of the series, and to Mr J. Lee, Fellow of Peterhouse, Cambridge who read and criticised sections of the manuscript. I also wish to thank Dr T. O'Neill of the National Museum of Ireland for valuable suggestions and unfailing interest, and Fr Conor Ryan, St John's Waterford for the light he threw on aspects of Stuart government. There are two others without whom this book would not have been written: Sister John Dominici Condon, O.P., my patient typist, and Mr W. J. Connolly who launched the series. Of all who assisted the author in this volume it can be said that they displayed a generosity of helpful suggestions which makes Irish history a pleasant discipline wherein to work.

MARGARET MAC CURTAIN

Department of Modern Irish History
University College
Dublin

1 King of England and Lord of Ireland

Geographical divisions in the sixteenth century

The geographical position of Ireland was to become increasingly defined during the century of Atlantic exploration. It was not so much that the island lay in the direct path of the Atlantic voyagers as that the new map-makers revealed the coastline of Europe to itself and the inescapable physical setting of Ireland on the margins of the known world was seen to lie the length of a sea-channel from its nominal master, England. Within the island there was little known of its features outside the central region of administration bordering Dublin, known appropriately as 'The Pale'.

According to an entry in the *State Papers Henry VIII* dated 1541 Ireland was described in divisions of provinces, shires, and regions 'inhabited with the King's Irish enemies'. As depicted in sixteenth-century maps, about forty-three walled towns survived into this period. The English Pale, a narrow strip thirty miles deep behind Dublin and Drogheda encompassing modern County Dublin and parts of Kildare, Meath and Louth, together with a few out-lying towns, remained the effective centre of English administration. Dispatches to Henry VIII and Wolsey give the impression that the Pale was like a large stockade with a small number of closely guarded exits at its frontiers, the most important being the bridge at Leighlin in County Carlow. The rest of the country was in the hands of either Anglo-Irish nobility or Gaelic-Irish families.

A sixteenth-century map of Ireland

Munster, Leinster and parts of Connacht had undergone considerable changes associated with earlier colonisation settlements and were strongly marked by Norman Anglo-Irish characteristics. Ulster was isolated from the rest of the country by a series of rivers, lakes, forests and mountains. Save for the eastern coast of Down and Antrim it was Gaelic territory.

The early Tudors possessed no clear map of the country. The sixteenth century in England, however, witnessed a growing interest in the techniques of map-making which developed in the age of Elizabeth into professional cartography as England acquired overseas territory across the Atlantic. Henry VIII's knowledge of Ireland, then, was of a pre-map kind and of a fragmentary nature. Judging by the later mid-century maps, the concentration of topographical detail in certain areas such as the Pale and southern regions of the country and the paucity and inaccuracy of the cartographical information for the north and west of Ireland suggest that geographical knowledge of the whole country was acquired gradually from first-hand experience gained by military marches through conquered territory.

Even at the end of the century Boazio's map reflects faithfully the 'two' Irelands which had existed side by side for centuries, though by that time, Elizabeth's military cartographers had supplied the missing text. Certainly at the beginning of Henry's reign the Irish countryside on the north and west of the Shannon was closed in by great tracts of forest within which Gaelic society generated its own political, economic and social life with little reference to the Tudors. It was a regressive society but not, as we shall see, a static one. In the south and east where Norman methods of colonisation some centuries earlier had taken root the countryside showed evidence of feudal ways. It would not be incorrect to say that the early Tudors, Henry VII and Henry VIII, saw Ireland in terms of zones or regions of loyalty to the English Crown occupied by the descendants of the earlier settlers, the Kildare Geraldines being the foremost. In Munster the Desmond Geraldines and in Leinster beyond the Pale, the Butlers of Ormond were technically the king's subjects.

Mixed farming along manorial lines introduced by the Normans left its mark on the regions they occupied. Gradually their countryside became studded with stone-built manor houses and defensive tower-houses with farm villages centred around the church and mill. Beyond and round the zones of loyalty lived the Irish inhabitants. They lived in septs or extended family structures. Lands were allotted according to tanistry in the case of the Gaelic ruler, and according to gavelkind in relation to lesser landowners. By contrast with the Anglo-Irish regions the Gaelic lordships retained open farm clusters worked in rundale by families and kin groups. It was a pastoral mode of living. The *clachan* or clustered house group was the social unit in Gaelic Ireland and shared in fragmented ownership. The 'infield' situated near the *clachan* was divided into strips and tilled by the kin group. Beyond the infield stretched the grazing lands of the cattle and sheep, known as the 'outfield'. These were the moors, the hilly uplands, the shores of lakes and rivers like Lough Neagh, the Shannon Basin and the upper reaches of the Blackwater. Though towns were not a feature of the Gaelic countryside, their presence in nearby Anglo-Irish areas had assumed the functions of market centres for the native Irish who gradually settled beyond the main walls of the larger cities as at Limerick, Kilkenny and Galway. Sometimes they absorbed smaller inland towns into their own economy as with Fore or Castledermot. The seaboard towns remained in the possession of the Anglo-Irish but, protected by their walls, they enjoyed independence, and were prosperous and busy.

Ownership rights were vested in the sept but the native aristocracy consisted of a dominant minority who held the

4

better land and exerted sway over tributary septs. Like the Anglo-Irish magnates, at the beginning of the sixteenth century certain Gaelic families held power. Of these the O'Neills in three great branches predominated in Ulster. To a lesser degree the O'Donnells in West Ulster; the MacCarthys in South Munster; the O'Connors, the O'Byrnes and O'Tooles around the Pale; the Maguires in Fermanagh and the MacMahons and O'Reillys around Cavan, represented centres of Gaelic automony and possible future rebellion.

Henry VIII, Lord of Ireland

With the reign of Henry VII the connection between the English monarchy and the lordship of Ireland began to reflect the changing concept of Tudor kingship. Henry VII brought to the throne the characteristics of a renaissance ruler. He was shrewd and calculating. Parsimonious by nature, he was intelligent in the employment of his resources. His interest in diplomacy, in the keeping of records, and in the rendering of accounts of revenues prepared the way for a state bureaucracy, later to develop into departments of state. A tireless worker, he maintained his position by soliciting support from all sections of his people. He was sensitive to public opinion, yet he preserved the majesty of kingship.

His son inherited a position of power and pre-eminence which both he and his subjects acknowledged as springing from his rights and prerogatives as a monarch. Under Henry VIII the king's prerogative became the touchstone of his personal rule, capable of being invoked alike in the interests of state, and in his private concerns. The second Tudor was accomplished, handsome and flamboyant. He inherited a throne that was secure and he embodied for his people the aspirations of English king worship. His early reign was characterised by an adherence to the lines of government laid down by his father. Yet the new reign

5

brought notable shifts of statecraft. Where Henry VII had asserted royal supremacy by ruling alone, his son maintained that supremacy by governing with the aid of two great ministers, Wolsey and – after Wolsey's downfall – Cromwell.

Wolsey was first noticed by Henry VII but received most of his honours from Henry VIII. His rise to power was spectacular. From 1512 onwards he was first in the king's confidence. To him increasingly from 1515 to 1529 was entrusted the shaping and execution of foreign and domestic policies, the administration of the law, the control of finances, the reform of the Church, and finally the divorce negotiations. His failure to acquire the desired dispensation for Henry VIII coincided with the collapse of his foreign policy. The man who became Lord Chancellor, Cardinal, and papal Legate made his exit with a finality which closed a chapter of England's history.

There is no evidence that Henry VIII took any personal interest in Irish affairs in the first years of his reign. Since 1494 he had been nominally lieutenant of his Irish Lordship but Sir Edward Poynings and the earl of Kildare between them dominated Irish politics. It was, however, an Indian summer to be terminated by the king's good pleasure.

The Kildares

Henry VII had not tested the strength of the Gaelic and Anglo-Irish lords in Ireland. Though the three earls, Kildare, Butler and Desmond dominated the southern parts of Ireland politically and economically, the interdependence between them as overlords and the surrounding Irish lords was noticeable in the spread of the Irish language and in the prominent position held by the Brehon in the administration of Irish law in, for example, the Palatinate court of the Butlers. The employment of gallowglasses and kerns was widespread. The peaceful custom of fosterage was common. In most respects the Gaelic revival had reached its zenith, but Irish society at the beginning of the sixteenth century was a backward-looking one.

It is doubtful if the great House of Kildare exercised in reality the powers extended to them by the first Tudor monarchs. The strength and impotence of Kildare's position were demonstrated during the deputyship of Sir Edward Poynings 1494–1496. This brief period foreshadowed the new regime of the Tudors. The English Deputy appointed the king's men to the great offices. He held a parliament which proceeded to restore the rights of the Crown and to annul legislation of the previous parliament. His new legislation, the ninth act of that parliament, Poynings Law, was to have profound repercussions on Irish parliamentary history for centuries to come. Potentially, if not in reality it ended the independence of the Pale administrators and, like the Tudor English parliament, reduced the role of the Irish parliament to one of servility.

Though the great earl of Kildare resumed office as lord deputy with much prestige after the Poynings interlude, his celebrated authority was now wielded in the name of the king. The invocation of the title 'king' however meaningless at first, gathered majesty with successive Tudor reigns. Garret Mór, the eighth earl of Kildare died in office as lord deputy in 1513. His son was his successor in office. Garret Óg's confirmation as lord deputy came a few months before Wolsey's assumption of control in England. Almost from the beginning Wolsey did not disguise his animosity towards the lord deputy and the rule of Garret Óg was punctuated by manifestations of authority which finally ushered in a new order.

Relations between Henry VIII and Garret Óg in the first years of the latter's deputyship were tranquil. There were visits of Garret Óg to the English Court and to his various English relatives. (He had married Elisabeth Zouch as his third wife.) There were occasional exchanges of gifts on Garret Óg's side, gifts of falcons and wolf-hounds; on the king's side, that of gunpowder. In general the lord deputy was granted full powers to hold parliament and to exercise wide jurisdiction throughout Ireland.

Yet King Henry was not without information on his Irish possessions. Under the patent of 1496 the position of Irish chancellor and chief justice of the King's Bench were reserved appointments. Within the Pale the king had power to nominate to ecclesiastical appointments. Beyond the Pale he had a constant source of information in the Butlers, loyal adherents of the Lancastrians in the previous century and in the sixteenth century to be called into closer familial bonds with the Tudors through Anne Boleyn.

By 1515 the new mood was perceptible. The appointment of John Kite as archbishop of Armagh a short time before was significant. An Englishman, he was one of Wolsey's circle and he kept the lord chancellor fully informed. Kite intimated that His Majesty's Irish lordships were much in need of the king's 'civility'. Gaelic practices had crept into local government, and Sir William Darcy, the ambitious under-treasurer of Fitzgerald's administration reinforced the allegations. In the summer of 1515 the Irish lord deputy was summoned before the King's Council at Greenwich to answer the charges. His explanations satisfied Henry and Garret Óg returned to Ireland with greatly increased powers. The following March, Garret Óg was granted a new patent empowering him to appoint his own chancellor and chief justice.

In the following years Garret Óg was left to his own devices. Kite returned to England. Darcy was dismissed from the Deputy's Council. The death of the earl's English wife, Elisabeth Zouch, withdrew him from English society. He turned his attention to Irish matters and in particular to his feud with his brother-in-law, Piers Roe, earl of Ormond. Previously Henry had shown himself well disposed to the Ormond family when he had exercised his influence on behalf of Sir Thomas Boleyn, one of the heir's male of the defunct earl of Ormond, Thomas. As yet Henry had not got involved with the Boleyn daughters. Besides he did not care for Piers Roe. There was nothing to warn Garret Óg that the growing rivalry between brothers-in-law might have unpleasant consequences for himself.

Among the resources of the Tudors was their ability to collect information. Both Henry and Wolsey followed the intrigues of the earl of Desmond with the king of France while noting at the same time the intimacy between Garret Óg and the earl of Desmond, just when the elements of a power struggle between Francis I and the newly-elected Emperor Charles V were becoming apparent. England's decision to support Charles V coincided with Henry's desire according to his Memo of 1519 to 'devise how Ireland may be reduced and restored to good order and obedience'.

In the autumn of 1519 the Irish lord deputy was again called to England to defend his actions. The mutual dislike between Kildare and Wolsey became evident on this occasion and hot words ensued. The episode resulted in the appointment of Thomas Howard, earl of Surrey, as lieutenant, a position not filled as such since 1460.

Surrey was an apt choice. A member of the Norfolk family, he had been Lord Admiral and was an experienced soldier. Ostensibly his mission to Ireland was to be a peaceful one but Henry's renowned dispatch to Surrey in 1520 sets the tone for all future Tudor conquests. Though Surrey was ordered to bring the king's dominion to a state of submission, it must be 'by sober waies, politique driftes, and amiable persuasions ... (rather) than by rigorous dealing, comminacious, or any other inforcement by strength or violence ... The King expects to get lands back which he had wrongfully lost, he does not wish to oppose injustice by injustice'. The dispatch goes on to add significantly: 'And it may be said unto them in good manner that like as we being their sovereign lord and prince though of our absolute power we be above the laws yet we will in no wise take anything from them that righteously appertains to them so of good congruence they be bound both by law fidelities and allegiance to restore unto us our own.' This was the son of Henry VII speaking with the certainty with which later he would invoke the royal prerogatives in the 1530s.

Surrey in Ireland entered upon a round of brilliant but ephemeral submissions. He reached agreements with Con O'Neill and Hugh O'Donnell. He invaded the fastnesses of Leix and Offaly, and after months of attack and counter-retaliation he received the doubtful submission of O'Carroll, O'More and O'Connor with such pledges as they offered. He established contacts with the Butlers, with the earl of Desmond, with MacCarthy Mór and MacCarthy Reagh.

It proved expensive. 'I and the treasurer with all the captains of the king's retinues here have not amongst us all £20 in money', Surrey wrote to Wolsey after four months of summer campaigning. The cost of the Irish wars began to be discussed in the King's Council and Henry's reply was firm: such an expense (£16,000 p.a. from the English Treasury) for the defence of the four Irish shires could not be entertained. Six months later Surrey's considered reply came. It indicated the general direction that Tudor policy in Ireland should take if a complete conquest was contemplated. Ireland would need an army of over 5,000 men whose billeting and financing would have to be subsidised from England. Castles and towns would be necessary as the conquest progressed. English settlers would be required 'to set the Irish to labour on the land'.

Surrey was on edge to depart from Ireland. 'I have continued here one year and a half, to your grace's great charges and to mine undoing for I have spent all that I might make', he complained bitterly to Wolsey then at Calais. Complaints about Surrey's moodiness found their way to Henry in letters. Surrey was recalled and it was agreed to give Sir Piers Butler the deputyship. Surrey returned briefly to Dublin in the spring of 1522 and supervised the assumption of office by Butler. His departure rounded off an important experiment in active Tudor intervention in Ireland.

Surrey's brief period of ruling Ireland brought to light a number of submerged considerations for Henry. Henceforth any realistic policy of intervention would have to take cognisance of financial as well as of military aspects. In this instance finance proved to be the weightiest factor in the decision not to proceed with an English lieutenancy. Implicit in Surrey's recall was the idea of future 'enterprise', and in Surrey's dispatches the first hint of future colonisation appeared. The pattern of Surrey's campaign was to be applied in various arrangements throughout the following century with much the same results.

The Butlers of Ormond

The senior line of the House of Ormond expired with Thomas, the seventh earl, in 1515. A cadet branch, the Butlers of Polestown, had deputised for the earl Thomas who was an absentee in England. This office was conveyed formally by deed to Edmund MacRichard of Polestown, to his son James, and to his grandson, Piers. The Butlers of Polestown had – in defiance of the Statutes of Kilkenny – married Irish wives, and the marriage between James Butler and Sabina Kavanagh was for long a celebrated law case. Their son was Piers Roe who assumed the title of earl of Ormond on the death of the seventh earl, Thomas. Piers Roe applied himself assiduously to proving the validity of his parents' marriage and to demonstrating that the Butler lands had been entailed by the fourth earl to heirs male. For a time his claims were not fully accepted by Henry VIII.

'Sir Pierce Butler, pretending himself to be Earl of Ormond', Henry wrote to Surrey in 1521.

The earl Thomas had left two daughters. Anne married Sir Thomas St Leger and Margaret married a rich and influential knight with merchant connections in the city of London, Sir William Boleyn. The daughters acquired possession of the English estates but for over a decade, Sir Piers Roe fought and eventually won succession to the Irish property. Sir William Boleyn who married Margaret Butler was the grandfather of Mary and Anne Boleyn, who in succession, attracted the affections of Henry VIII. Their father, Sir Thomas Boleyn, was created Viscount Rochford in 1525, and two years later was given the title earl of Wiltshire and Ormond. Though the ambitious Boleyns never ceased to contest the Irish lands, they were resisted by the equally ambitious and more resourceful Sir Piers Roe. His appointment as deputy in 1522 was a signal mark of favour and was accompanied by the title of earl of Ormond.

Geographically the new deputy, Butler, was at a disadvantage. Entrance to and from the Pale ran through the territory of his rival, Garret Óg Fitzgerald. Kildare arrived back in Ireland with his new wife Lady Elisabeth Grey towards the beginning of 1523. He was still smarting from the cross-examination to which Wolsey had subjected him in England. He had been imprisoned for a short period on charges of 'seditious practices, conspiracies and subtill draftes'.

His return was the signal for a period of active quarrelling between the two earls, the odds going to Kildare. Before two years had elapsed, Kildare was re-appointed deputy with Ormond as treasurer. It was a tacit admission of Kildare's power in Ireland. There was another urgent reason for the transfer of office. James, earl of Desmond had finally made a convention with the king of France. King Henry freed Ormond to guard the south and to watch

Desmond who had seized every opportunity to pillage Ormond's territories while the latter was deputy. For all practical purposes the Desmonds were independent sovereigns. Politically they were hostile to the Butlers. Traditionally they were anti-monarchical.

A long standing friendship between the Houses of Kildare and Desmond was now cemented by concerted antagonism towards the Butlers. Accordingly Kildare turned a blind eye on Desmond's continental intrigues. Wolsey again demanded Kildare's presence in London where he was retained though not in custody. Repercussions followed swiftly in Ireland. Kildare's son-in-law, O'Connor Offaly, captured the newly-appointed Lord Justice, Lord Delvin. Delvin was a close friend of Butler and the kidnapping greatly angered Wolsey. There was little he could do. The year was 1528.

Sometime within the previous year Henry VIII had signified to Wolsey his intention to marry Anne Boleyn, to make her his queen and have a legitimate heir. Charles V countered the request by making Pope Clement VII virtually his prisoner. Wolsey then prevailed on Henry and Francis I of France to declare war on the Emperor. This action vexed the English people, particularly the merchants, already exasperated by Wolsey's management of affairs. Henry VIII quick to catch the mood of his subjects, allowed the war to come to a standstill and a truce was declared. The king's confidence in Wolsey was being steadily eroded by the active dislike of Anne Boleyn, and that of her patron, Norfolk (better known in Irish history as Surrey); yet the seriousness of Wolsey's position was not apparent.

There were, however, straws in the wind for the discerning in Ireland. Sir Thomas Boleyn, father of Anne, acquired in February 1528 the title of earl of Ormond, to which was later added that of Wiltshire, together with certain Butler lands in Ireland. Sir Piers Butler, outwardly amicable to the proposal agreed to exchange his Ormond title for that of Ossory. Though he was reappointed deputy, his prestige had diminished along with that of his patron, Wolsey.

One of the first to sense the direction of the new English policy was James, earl of Desmond, who now began to make overtures to Charles V. But Butler's inability to discipline Desmond convinced Henry VIII that temporising was dangerous. In June 1529, Henry Duke of Richmond, the illegitimate son of Henry VIII, was made lieutenant of Ireland. The significance of the appointment lay in its consequences. Henceforth the Tudors, with rare exceptions, were prepared to maintain an Englishman in Ireland as their representative. With the new appointment went a re-shuffle in the Dublin administration. The king established a council of officials to offset the personal rule of a Kildare. Sir William Skeffington, master of the king's ordnance was sent over as a special commissioner to assess the military situation. King Henry had set up the beginnings of the bureaucracy which was to become increasingly a mark of Tudor government in Ireland.

With the fall of Wolsey, an influential group took their places around Henry VIII. These were Thomas More, the new Lord Chancellor, the dukes of Norfolk and Suffolk in first rank, with the bishops, Stephen Gardiner and John Fisher. In the background were Thomas Cromwell and Thomas Cranmer, the Cambridge divine. Henry was set on a course which led to schism and to royal supremacy. The years 1529-34 were momentous years for England. Parliament sat and a revolution in government took place peacefully.

In Ireland the same span of years witnessed the eclipse of the House of Kildare. When Skeffington had restored a measure of order the king allowed Kildare to return to Ireland without office after a prolonged sojourn in England. There Garret Óg had successfully worked up a coalition in his favour consisting of Lord Leonard Grey, his wife's brother, and Wiltshire, father of Anne Boleyn. The king's trust seemed justified. Skeffington and Kildare set about restoring order jointly but soon there were complaints that Kildare was undermining the authority of Skeffington. Skeffington was appointed deputy. It was one of the last appointments Norfolk made before Thomas Cromwell assumed control of affairs in Ireland. It was unsuccessful and Henry reappointed Kildare in 1532 for the last time.

Two intensive decades of warfare and politics had taken their toll of Kildare. In December 1532 he was wounded in battle. 'He never after enjoyed his limbs, nor delivered his words in good plight', was how Stanihurst, the Tudor historian, recorded his decline. Garret Óg's domination over Irish affairs was gone. In Henry's eyes the problem was how to replace him.

Thomas Cromwell had become the key-figure in the Tudor government. Almost immediately he interested himself in Ireland. The new Master of the Rolls, John Alen, was one of Cromwell's appointments and was given the task of reporting on Kildare. It was an easy task. All Kildare's enemies were on his back. Butler and his henchmen, the two Cowleys, kept up a continual flow of complaints to Cromwell. Skeffington passed on his sources to Cromwell. Eventually allegations of possible treason against King Henry took an ominous note. It was reported that Kildare was transferring the royal ordnance from Dublin Castle to Maynooth. He was ordered to England and was permitted to leave his son, Lord Offaly, in charge as Lord Justice. With foreboding Garret Óg left for London where he was immediately charged with using the king's artillery for the defence of his own castles.

The Insurrection of Silken Thomas

The suddenness of the rebellion which followed Kildare's commitment to the Tower can be explained by the hastiness of his son to accept the rumours that his father had been executed. Stanihurst, with hindsight, described Lord Offaly as 'of nature flexible and kind, very soon carried where he fancied, easily with submission appeased, hardly with stubborness weighed, in matters of importance a headlong hotspur . . .' The dramatic incident of Silken Thomas's ride into Dublin where he flung down the sword of state before the surprised Councillors has been appreciated by Irish historians. There were, however, a number of wider issues which made the rebellion of Silken Thomas more than a colourful medieval episode.

Though the force of the rebellion was quickly spent, the support afforded Offaly by the gentlemen of the Pale and by O'Neill, MacMurrough, O'More, O'Connor and O'Byrne was a significant coalition for possible war in Ireland. Its continuance into the later Geraldine League which conspired to protect the only survivor of the Kildare House, a boy of twelve, may also be seen as a new consciousness to resist Tudor domination. Butler alone stood out in his support of his new protector Cromwell, and by an inversion of memory later on, he was rewarded for his loyalty to the Crown.

Undoubtedly the Reformation in England, though not a cause of the Irish rebellion, helped to form attitudes. In June 1534 Cowley wrote to Cromwell: 'The said Earl's son (Lord Offaly), kinsmen and adherents do make their avaount and boast that they be of the pope's sect and band, and him will they serve against the King and all his partakers'. Substantial rumours were circulating in the summer of 1534 that an imperial army sent by Charles V at the instigation of the earl of Desmond would assist the Fitzgeralds in the opposition to the king. The isolation of King Henry cut off by communication from, yet participating in, European affairs made any combination between the pope, a European monarch, and the king's Irish subjects matter for urgent action in Ireland, a pattern which was to repeat itself in varying forms throughout the following two centuries.

The Geraldine league

The execution of Thomas, tenth earl of Kildare (his father, Garret Óg, had died in December 1534) and of his five uncles at Tyburn was an act of unusual harshness. Though it could be interpreted as Henry's determination to exterminate all who opposed royal dominion, its immediate consequence was to consolidate rebellion in Munster. The new earl of Desmond, James Fitzgerald, combined with O'Brien, and with many of the Anglo-Irish of Munster to resist Lord Grey, the soldier-deputy who had replaced Kildare. Grey, with Butler's help had temporarily succeeded in invading Thomond but was crippled by lack of money and by threatened mutiny in his army. He opened negotiations with the Munster rebels. The knowledge that his nephew, the young Gerald, half-brother to Silken Thomas, was in hiding with the powerful O'Brien led him to negotiate further. He finally returned to Dublin with little accomplished and with heavy financial drains.

Lord Leonard Grey, a brilliant campaigner, demonstrated in the following years his ability to open up the fastnesses of Gaelic Ireland by his systematic, indeed ingenious, exploration of region after region. His midland campaigns of 1537 set the standard for Tudor warfare in Ireland. Thomas Cromwell, however was a man of the inkpots. He preferred the compilation of information as a preliminary to policy-making. Already the dissolution of the monasteries in Ireland had been introduced, and in 1537 a commission under Sir Anthony St Leger was empowered 'to examine the offices and behaviour as well of the Deputy as of all other of the King's Council; to enquire in what places the King's laws were obeyed; to survey the lands, as yet desolate, which had fallen to the Crown by the Act of Attainder, the Act of Suppression, and the Act of

Ireland about 1530

Absentees; to grant leases for twenty-one years to Englishmen and others of the King's faithful subjects who would encourage their tenants to "inhabit and manure the same"; the amount of the revenue, and the best means of collecting it; and to discharge as many of the soldiers as could be dismissed with safety'.

The immediate effect of the Report, compiled within the year, was to discredit the deputy. Grey was accused of cultivating the malcontents, and of co-operating in the restoration of the Kildares. The deep dislike that existed between Butler and Grey did not help the latter. Piers Butler had been restored to the title of Ormond and he and his son James stood high in favour. The Butlers were assiduous in keeping Henry informed, and were among the first to give news of a confederacy who were plotting in 1538 to restore Gerald Fitzgerald. Grey had never been able to clear himself of Geraldine sympathies; his sister, after all, was the mother of Gerald. Despite a swift military reconnoitre that brought him through Desmond, Thomond and Galway, thence to Roscommon, Athlone and Westmeath, his enemies renewed the charges, accusing him of allowing Gerald and his aunt to pass unmolested to the north. Still the king waited.

By 1539 the Geraldine Confederacy was a formidable league. Its real strength was concealed from Henry's government who feared a religious element in the cementing of loyalties. Alen, Master of the Rolls, reported to Cromwell: 'I suspect much our own country, what for the affection part of them bear to the Geraldines, and the favour that many hath to the Bishop of Rome, and his laws and errors, that they will either turn against us, or otherwise stand us in small stead . . .'

When the conspiracy was eventually revealed through the depositions of young Kildare's servant, it was of ambitious proportions. Though the restoration of Kildare was central to the Confederacy, significantly there was an intimation by Con O'Neill that he was willing to assume the kingship of Ireland.

The Confederacy never at any time represented a military threat to Grey. The defeat of the Ulster forces at Bellahoe was an event of some importance but, with the departure of the young Kildare for France, the Confederacy dissolved. Grey was recalled to England where he was charged with treason and executed.

With the fall of the Kildare House, and to a lesser extent with the execution of Lord Leonard Grey for treason, the English monarchy became a decisive force in Irish politics. The increasing watchfulness of Wolsey, and later of Cromwell, over the movements of Irish deputies was matched by a growing interest on Henry's part to intervene independently in Irish affairs. It was Henry who selected Grey, and later had him executed. It was Henry who reappointed Garret Óg and, stung by the threat of foreign intervention, it was Henry who initiated the combination of conquest and ecclesiastical reformation which was to characterise the Tudor efforts to subdue the island.

After 1535 the Tudor monarchy preferred to use its own agents. Succeeding deputies were obliged to be royal servants and they employed a council in Dublin which resembled that of Wales or the Council of the North. From then on the New English constituted a constant threat to the existing structure of Anglo-Irish administration in the Pale.

The rebellion of the Fitzgeralds coincided with the English Reformation which in turn set in motion the dissolution of the monasteries in Ireland. Long regarded as a turning point in Irish history because of its striking symbolism, 1534 was the year of high visibility in a set of circumstances beginning with the appointment of the earl of Surrey as lieutenant. What had emerged in the intervening years was the difficulty of resolving who was *de jure* ruler of Ireland. Technically the king of England was lord of Ireland through a Papal grant. With Henry constituted head of the English Church his claims in Ireland conflicted with the pope's authority there and his Dublin Council advised Henry to take the title of king of Ireland to dissipate 'the foolish opinion amongst them that the Bishop of Rome should be king of the same'.

2 Reformation and Supremacy

An Act of State

The events in England and in Ireland which brought about
the Henrician reformation in the 1530s were marked by
constitutional and legal innovations. Royal supremacy in
England was given statutory expression in the Reformation Parliament, 1529–1536; in Ireland it was embodied
in the Dublin Parliament 1536–7. Wolsey's replacement as
primate in England was Cranmer, the architect of the
Anglican Church, Henry's personal choice. The English
Augustinian friar, George Browne who had been active in
supporting royal supremacy in England, was appointed by
Henry VIII to the See of Dublin in 1536 without sanction
of Rome. In Ireland the bureaucratic changes which
followed the Fitzgerald rebellion were consequential.
While not attaining the stature of the Tudor administrative revolution effected during the same decade in
England, the shaping policy was identical. In both countries
the dissolution of the monasteries was a contemporary
event, issuing from an act of state and signifying the
assumption of papal by royal interests in the financial
organisation of the Church within the realms of Henry
VIII. The similarities in procedure in the two countries
were noteworthy but the reality was as between substance
and shadow. In so far as the Henrician reformation in
Ireland represented a moral revolt against the relaxed
discipline of the late medieval Church, the impetus was
arrested by the ethnic divisions among the population, and

by the general unpreparedness of the Irish Church for the doctrinal changes then sweeping Europe. Where in England, the historian can speak of an 'old religion' and a 'new religion', in Ireland it is more accurate to describe an *Ecclesia inter Hibernos* and an *Ecclesia inter Anglos*, a division which from the beginning complicated any planned change by royal authority.

One of the long-term results of the Norman invasion was the partitioning of the Irish Church organisationally along ethnic lines. A line of division was inserted at various intervals from 1217 onwards into the structure of the Irish Church by means of prohibitions issued to prevent Irishmen from attaining ecclesiastical dignities in Norman areas. The Statutes of Kilkenny gave explicit form to this policy of ethnic division and with a severity intensified by fear of extinction English dioceses in Ireland were forced by law to preserve themselves from contamination with Irish ways of life. There existed side by side separate dioceses serving those who spoke the Irish language, and those who were defined as English-speaking. The struggle for ecclasiastical domination ran deeply. The diocese of Armagh was divided into two sections. The Archbishop of Armagh was nominally Fnglish or Anglo-Irish and resided at Termonfeckin or Dromiskin. The dean of Armagh was normally of Irish descent and he administered the Irish half of the diocese from Armagh. A similar cleavage ran through the religious orders in Ireland, most noticeable among the mendicant orders. The Austin Friars and the Dominicans were not permitted to attain the status of a full Irish province, but had to be content with the status of vicar-provincialship, dependent on English provinces. Though the Franciscans possessed an Irish province, it was divided into four 'custodies' of which three were given to the English-speaking friars, and the remaining custody at Nenagh was for the native Irish.

Technically the Irish Church bore a special relationship

to the king of England since the time of Henry II. In the intervening centuries legislation, either by way of canon law or by act of parliament, reiterated the ecclesiastical relationship that existed between the inhabitants of Ireland and the English monarch. The grant of Ireland made by Pope Adrian IV to the English kings carried with it overtones of expected allegiance and submission for the Irish. Popes Alexander II and Honorius III voiced similar sentiments and Pope John XXII issued a general excommunication against the Irish supporters of the Bruces. Papal sympathy for the king of England was one thing; papal sanction for royal ecclesiastical appointments was quite another matter. The disappearance of episcopal registers in Irish dioceses save those of Armagh during the fifteenth century make it difficult to record the state of the Irish Church but papal provisions became increasingly vexatious to the English monarchy and provides a clue why Henry VIII assumed the function of Head of the Church with such little hesitation. In Ireland any policy of uniformity was challenged by the existence, side by side, of an 'Irish' Church and an 'English' Church.

Ecclesia inter Hibernos

The Church in Gaelic Ireland was an elaborate network of occupations and relationships involving a hierarchy of functions which related back to the position of the various families within the sept. Central to the organisation of the Church in Gaelic parts of Ireland was the part played by the *coarbs* and *erenaghs*.

Originally the term *comharba* signified heir or successor to the highest office in a great monastery or abbey. By the beginning of the sixteenth century, it was a term loosely applied to a position occupied by either a cleric or a layman, and to offices ranging from that of bishops or archbishops as in the case of Tuam or Emly, to that of prior or abbot of a religious house in a Gaelic 'country'. However the title, *erenagh*, could just as likely belong to the layhead of an ecclesiastical collegiate institution as in Scattery Island or Devenish or to the rector, (whether lay or cleric of a particular place), or to a title inherited by a family like that of the O'Farrellys at Drumlane, Co. Cavan. Over the centuries the name, *erenagh*, came to be applied to the person, lay or clerical, or even to the family, to whom certain Church lands were handed over in exchange for certain rents and services to the bishops. *Erenagh* land bore a faint resemblance to the monastic granges; in both cases, by the time of Henry VIII, they were no longer associated with particular monasteries as is evident from Inquisition records and Fiants.

By the end of the fifteenth century the occupation of a *coarb* was mainly that of steward of church lands with certain obligations such as the payment of dues and services to the local church or monastery. The *coarb* was an educated man, with a knowledge of canon and brehon law, a writing knowledge of Latin and Irish. He was a recorder, annalist and sometimes a poet. The *coarb* was bound to hospitality and could in many places claim benefit of clergy. He was subject to episcopal visitation and normally he had a consultative vote on matters of church policy, finance and administration. The office of *coarb* was closely linked to that of the sept families. By the time of Henry VIII the law of succession by tanistry was being abandoned in favour of primogeniture and the custom of appointing a member of the same family as the previous holder had by then become a condition.

The offices of *coarb* and *erenagh* were closely identified in late medieval Ireland. Socially, the status of the *coarb* was higher and his title more hereditary than that of *erenagh*. The name 'coarb of Ciaran' for example evoked long associations in people's memories, whereas the 'erenagh of Tulach Aoibhinn' conveyed simply the limits of the office-holder. In cases where the *erenagh* had become, by custom, a layman with ecclesiastical duties, he tended to belong to a landed farming class with certain church privileges.

There were other functionaries in the Church in Gaelic Ireland who had a precise social identification by the opening decades of the sixteenth century. The *terminer* was the occupier of certain church or monastic lands, usually at a distance from the monastery or friary. Occcasionally the *terminer* enjoyed the status of *coarb* or *erenagh* but in the case of the friars, the *terminer* was selected from among the friars and was subject to the superior of his own friary. In sixteenth-century Ireland the *terminer* was to play a hidden but significant role as priest in areas where a monastery was suppressed but the law had not yet caught up with the confiscation of the 'term' or '*limes*'.

The *duchasach* or *nativus* was originally a serf, then a tenant at will of a small parcel of land allocated for the support of a chapel of ease. Eventually he could aspire to becoming a small landed proprietor.

By the reformation decade an elaborate arrangement of fiscal transactions and church land tenures were administered by laymen in Gaelic Ireland. The *coarbs* and *erenaghs* were at the centre of the financial system. They were the bishops' providers, collectors, syndics and bankers. The mensal lands of the clergy – either those owned by them or directly occupied by them – were small but the 'censual' lands were considerable. These latter were the church lands occupied by *coarbs, erenaghs, terminers* and *duchasaigh*.

Territorially any discipline imposed by Henry VIII depended firstly on the subduing of the Irish regions and on the abolishing of the special ecclesiastical functions within the church in Gaelic Ireland. It was a task which baffled Tudor land-assessors for many decades. Almost a century later, Sir John Davies with his shrewd legal intelligence observed that 'the like (*coarbs* and *erenaghs*) are not to be found in any other part of Christendom, nor in Ireland neither, but only in the countries that are mere Irish'.

Ecclesia inter Anglos

Even before the Statutes of Kilkenny had decreed ecclesiastical division between native Irish and Anglo-Normans, the lines of separation had been worked out in parish boundaries, in tithing lands, in monasteries and in church appointments. The clear distinction between men of the Irish and men of the English tongue affected the episcopacy, the parish clergy and religious orders.

In England during the middle ages the appointment of bishops was practically conferred by the crown and subsequent confirmation by the papacy was in the form of ratification. In Ireland the papacy claimed a general over-lordship of the whole island and Irish sees were habitually filled by papal provision. By custom Englishmen were appointed to the important sees, Armagh, Dublin, Meath and Kildare. It was a tacit admission by the Holy See of the political importance of these sees to the king, and their incumbents had seats in the House of Lords and took their places in the privy council. In 1494, for instance, the archbishops of Armagh and Dublin and the bishops of Meath and Kildare together with the sheriffs of the four shires were ordered to repair the fortresses on the borders of the Pale. Englishmen were often appointed to the sees of Cork, Limerick and Waterford, cities predominantly Anglo-Irish or English. Absenteeism was frequent and during the fifteenth century a growing number of English monks and friars obtained papal provisions to Irish dioceses while remaining in England as suffragan bishops in one or other diocese there. Abuses of all kinds developed and the late medieval Irish church was ill-provided with a hierarchy capable of remedying these grave abuses.

The parish clergy represented a lower strata of Anglo-Irish society in Ireland. Many of them were peasant farmers: 'They cowde more by the plough rustical than by the lucre of the plough celestial', declared the Report of the State of Ireland, 1515.

The richest benefices were attached to the religious houses which in the general wretchedness that prevailed in the fifteenth century, leased out property as well as farmed out services in return for revenue. Henry VIII may have been writing tongue in cheek to Butler, earl of Ossory in 1534 when he complained 'the said Bishop of Rome commonly hath preferred, by his provisions, to the administration and goverance of them vile and vicious persons, unlearned, being murderers, thieves, and of other unjust maintenance therein, sometimes do expel the rightful incumbents, and other seasons, by force of secular power, do put the true patrons from their patronage'. There is no need to doubt the sincerity of Henry's zeal for reform; in general the Irish church experienced the same relaxed discipline of the late medieval Church as did England or Scotland. What was not apparent in 1534 was that the Irish Church still possessed considerable vitality and as a Church in association with the Roman Pontiff was capable of retaining the attachment of many of its followers.

First intimations of reform

The supplanting of papal by royal supremacy in England was accomplished in a series of swift events. The progress of the divorce suit and the trial of Catherine in 1529 was followed by the 'Submission of the Clergy' in 1532 from which it was but a step to the repudiation of papal jurisdiction in 1533 and to the final acknowledgement by Act of state in 1534 that Henry 'shall be taken, accepted and regarded' as Supreme Head of the Church of England. It brought to a close the first phase of the Henrician Reformation and became the starting point of its second phase. There was no going back.

It was at this juncture, 1534, that Ireland received its first intimations that Henry VIII intended to carry out the same kind of reformation by the same due processes in law. The Geraldine rebellion was not a religious revolt but it made possible the strategies by which the Henrician reformation was imposed upon the Irish church.

Sometime between 1529–34 personal rule by lord deputy had given way to a system of bureaucratic government. Outwardly Garret Óg was getting his last chance but the appointment of Richmond, Henry's son, as lieutenant of Ireland ushered in a new method of ruling in Dublin. The establishment of a 'secret council' in 1529 composed of the Chancellor, Archbishop John Alen, the Englishman Rawson, and Patrick Bermingham the chief justice was overshadowed somewhat by Skeffington's arrival as the king's special commissioner. Its main task was then 'to represent the place, Rome, and the authority of the King's Deputy there' and the secret council continued to function after Skeffington's departure. Cromwell whose star was rising found it particularly useful as a source of information. John Alen was appointed Master of the Rolls and became Cromwell's chief informant. Step by step the Geraldine downfall was accompanied by the building up of an English-controlled executive in Dublin which made possible the introduction of Henry's reform plans for Ireland.

The first discernible step towards reformation was taken at the end of May 1534 when Butler, earl of Ossory undertook to consolidate the south midlands against the earl of Desmond and to repudiate papal authority within his sphere of control. Almost simultaneously the *Ordinances for the Government of Ireland* appeared from the king's printer. These were a series of directives for the new deputy; in reality, Henry's manifesto of his new policy. The Dublin administration was directed to set aside papal provisions and papal jurisdiction, following the recent legislation passed in the English parliament. These were to be legislated against in a forthcoming Irish parliament. What Henry was really stating was that wherever royal dominion was challenged by papal dominion in his territories, he was not prepared to tolerate the resulting confusion.

No revolution occurred over Henry's bid for control of episcopal appointments in Ireland. Yet the incident of the slaying of Archbishop John Alen, Wolsey's vice-legate in Dublin, by the followers of Lord Offaly (Silken Thomas) was not a trivial one. It precipitated the Fitzgeralds into revolt against Henry VIII and Lord Offaly made the gesture of appealing to Rome and to Charles V for help in what he described as a crusade against the heretical Henry VIII. The religious element never became a serious threat and the rebellion was soon quelled. Henry, however, used the occasion to introduce his reform measures.

The appointment of Dr George Browne, the English Augustinian, was a royal one. Cromwell had employed him as visitator-general of the mendicant orders in England and he was an enthusiastic promotor of royal supremacy. His appointment to Dublin rather than to the primatial see of Armagh was a recognition of the traditional importance of the Dublin metropolitan. In the past the two offices of archbishop of Dublin and lord chancellor had been embodied in the one person, usually an Englishman. Browne was to proceed in the management of spiritual matters as the king's chief representative. Directions for his election as successor to Archbishop Alen were sent to the cathedral chapters in Dublin, Christ Church and St Patrick's. This was duly accomplished and in March George Browne was consecrated archbishop of Dublin by Cranmer. His arrival in Dublin in July 1536 immersed him immediately in the affairs of the parliament which had got under way in May 1536.

The Reformation Parliament

On May Day 1536 the Reformation Parliament opened in Dublin. That same year the English Reformation Parliament dissolved, having passed a programme of intense and radical legislation within the span of its existence. Like its greater counterpart, the Dublin parliament was to prove the most important of the Tudor period. The composition of its members, the body of legislation enacted, the use made of Poynings Law and of a selected executive demonstrated the consummate skill reached by Henry and Cromwell in achieving planned change in the mid-thirties.[1]

Little is known of the method of election. A hint is given in a report cited in the State Papers describing how the members of the Council including Ormond made it their business to be present at the election of the burgesses and knights of the shires 'to the intent that such persons of gravity and discretion may be elected, as of likelihood, of wilfulness, of sensuality, contrary to equity or reason, should not stick in the King's causes'.[2] According to Philip Wilson it is likely that nine counties, and between twenty and thirty boroughs, sent representatives to the lower house.[3] The Irish parliament at this time allowed for representatives of the lower clergy, two from each diocese, known as clerical proctors, to take their seats in the Commons. In the upper house were the lords temporal and spiritual.

The parliament, to some extent, was peripatetic. The lord deputy, Grey, was campaigning in the south and parliament followed him to Cashel, Kilkenny and to Limerick. By mid-September parliament was back in Dublin and opposition began to manifest itself. The sittings were prorogued at the end of the month and the following January the third session was held briefly, terminating in confusion. In May 1537 parliament reassembled for some weeks and the final session was held in late autumn of that year.

The measures of the Irish parliament were in the main copied from England but whereas in England, the parliament and the people rallied to, and became the accomplices of the king in the defence of Royal Supremacy as the international situation darkened, no such cohesion of national sentiment took place in Ireland. For one thing the introduction of Henry's ecclesiastical legislation in the Irish parliament only affected the colonists as yet. How clear they were on the obligations placed upon them by assuming a position in the dispute between monarch and pope is a debated point among historians. Opposition proved to be of a complex pattern obscured further by the exertions of an English-dominated executive and by the crippling powers of Poynings Law.

The authority of Henry over Church and state seems to have been acknowledged willingly enough. The speed with which the Supremacy legislation passed in the first session is testified by the report of Brabazon, the vice-treasurer, and by others.

Brabazon was soon reporting unease among the clerical proctors who seem to have been the only visible group who dissented from the enactment of royal supremacy. In the second and subsequent sessions opposition in the commons manifested itself in dissatisfaction over the Monasteries Bill, in defeating bills for customs duties and for imposing a land tax on the colonists (the Twentieth Bill). Personalities emerged in the parliament. Patrick Barnewall became the spokesman for the commons opposition and did rather well out of his protest. Robert Cowley was the indefatigable, and indeed spiteful, relayer of gossip about the colony to London. The subterfuges of John Alen, Master of the Rolls, and Gerald Aylmer as members of the Dublin Council charged by Henry and Cromwell to get the reform legislation through the Irish parliament come to light under scrutiny.

Early in 1537 when rumours of a Geraldine restoration

were flying, opposition was further evidenced by the spiritual lords in the upper house. Hitherto they had remained apathetic and silent despite the threats to them of the Monasteries and the Twentieth Bills. They proceeded to take a stand on the rights of the clerical proctors in parliament who had previously proved an embarrassment to the smooth running of the commons and were declared, in accordance with English procedure, to be an anomaly and therefore capable of elimination. Opposition, in fact, collapsed when confronted with four royal commissioners headed by Sir Anthony St Leger. These had been sent across by Henry to hold parliament, to survey royal lands and to lease confiscated estates. Henry also dispatched reproofs to Archbishop Browne and Bishop Staples of Meath for their tardiness in rallying the lords spiritual. They held office he reminded them during good behaviour.

That it was not an organised opposition is clear from the internal evidence. The clerical proctors were the most clear-sighted group in their grasp of the implications of royal supremacy in the first session. The group headed by Patrick Barnewall was motivated by self-interest and did not constitute a genuine opposition when confronted with the monastic spoils. The lords spiritual from whom opposition in the matters of royal supremacy and the Monasteries' Bill could be expected were a colourless group who subsided quickly before the concerted stand of the commissioners. It was not necessarily a 'managed' parliament. Yet the credit for carrying through measures which changed radically the relations between church and state in Ireland went in first place to Henry and Cromwell, and then to the council in Dublin.

In all the Irish Reformation Parliament passed about forty-two statutes in the relatively short sittings of its span. A small number of bills were concerned with social and economic problems within the colony. Legislation was passed, for instance, against marrying Irishmen in accordance with English policy since the statutes of Kilkenny. Where Irishmen failed to take the oath of succession such marriages were declared treasonable. A bill was passed endeavouring to restrict weirs on the rivers Barrow and Boyne. However the main legislation of the Irish Reformation Parliament was ecclesiastical, and severed relationship between Irish Catholics and the papacy. For some time yet its repercussions were not felt. The dissolution of the monasteries was a material reminder of the new order of relationships.

The dissolution of the monasteries

In Ireland, as in England, the dissolution of the monasteries was initiated with a suddenness which indicated a whole change of mood from the occasional acts of spoliation which were recorded in the late middle ages. Unlike England no royal visitation was carried out beforehand nor was a report on the state of religious living submitted to parliament. The main objective of the Irish suppression legislation seems to have been to legalise a process already begun by commission under the great seal in June 1535. The central reason for the dissolution was as in England to endow the Crown.

It was a gradual transfer of property within the Anglo-Irish parts of Ireland, accompanied by a developing mechanism of legal inquiry which was later employed in the Gaelic areas and in the plantation schemes. The *Fiants* for the reign of Henry VIII supply many details about the techniques employed by the commissioners, the extent and valuation of the properties surveyed, and occasionally they supply a hint of estate management. Watermills and salmon weirs were noted. Orchards, arable acreage, gardens, moor and pasture lands were listed. Archdall's account of the suppression of St Wolstan's near Leixlip and the grant of its immense properties to John Alen, Master of the Rolls, gives a picture of rural prosperity within the Pale. 'Richard Weston was the last prior, and this year, on the feast of St Simon and St Jude, 28th King Henry VIII, he was seized on the site of the abbey with four gardens, four parks, eight orchards, and six cottages, with their appurtenances, all situate within the said site, and adjoining the river Liffey; also of certain parcels of lands, being the demesne of the priory.' There follows a long descriptive list of pasture, meadow and woodlands, water-mills, and various properties.[4]

A small number of houses were suppressed in the years 1538–39; by 1540 almost all the religious houses in the Pale, in the Butler territories, and in the chief towns and cities of the south had been dissolved, and St Leger was entrusted with the task of taking surveys of the monastic property then decreed, by the suppression, to be royal property. By an Order of the lord deputy and council to the earl of Desmond in 1542 a commission was to be set up 'to take inventories and dissolve and put in safe custody all religious houses in the counties of Limerick, Cork, Kerry and Desmond' but in practice religious houses in Gaelic areas were, for the time being, left undisturbed.

The suppression of religious houses in Ireland was a slow process and the *Fiants* of successive Tudor monarchs bear testimony to the absorption of monastic lands first into the hands of layowners and later into the schemes of the new colonisers. Patrick Barnewall overcame his misgivings over the Monasteries Bill to the extent of becoming the lessee of well-endowed religious properties including the convent of Grace Dieu in north County Dublin. In the same year as he moved into Grace Dieu he acquired the extensive lands and site of the Carmelite friary at Knocktopher, County Kilkenny. The Butlers steadily augmented their property right through the century by acquiring the lease or freehold of religious estates within their territories. In the Gaelic areas religious houses like the abbey of Bangor nominally lapsed to the Crown in the reign of Henry VIII and were retained by neighbouring lords until the conquest of Ulster made plantation possible. Turlough Luineach O'Neill, for example, had a clause inserted into his treaty with Essex, June 1575, granting him 'all the lands of monasteries, abbacies and of other spiritual buildings within the said precincts' of the lands granted to him. With the reign of James I came the consistent attempt to vest all lands in the Crown, a task eventually accomplished by the Act of Settlement in 1662. The suppression of the monasteries in the Irish colony did little to advance the revenues of the king in that part of his territories. It was, however, the first decisive bid for the eventual take over of the land of Ireland.

Archbishop Browne's activities

Meanwhile the new archbishop of Dublin, Dr George Browne, found himself surrounded by difficulties of a concrete nature. His irritability as an individual and his lack of familiarity with his new diocese alienated him from his clergy. He quarrelled bitterly with Bishop Staples, the Lincolnshire born bishop of Meath who supported Henry's reform policy and controlled the bishops in the Irish House of Lords. Browne's enthusiasm for royal supremacy which issued in directives to use a public form of prayer renouncing the pope's authority was largely ignored. He complained to Cromwell in a letter of 9 January 1539: 'Before that our most dread sovereign was declared to be, as he ever was indeed, Supreme Head over the Church committed unto his princely care, they that could and would, very often till the right Christians were weary of them, preach after the old sort and fashion, will not now once open their lips in any pulpit for the manifestation of the same.'

The repudiation of papal jurisdiction and its substitution by royal supremacy provoked less opposition than might have been expected. Eight bishops and two archbishops, those of Cashel and Tuam, had taken the Oath of Supremacy by the beginning of 1539. But the passing of the Six Articles later that year was a serious setback for the Lutheran element within the English Church. Henry VIII had constantly professed his adherence to orthodoxy and became more repressive in extinguishing heresy as the years went by. Within his Church a group with whom Cromwell and Archbishop Cranmer were associated favoured Lutheran doctrines and were for carrying the reformation beyond the rupture with the papacy and the suppression of the monasteries. Up to 1539 compromise had been possible between this progressive party and the more traditional and conservative group of which Bishop Gardiner and the duke of Norfolk were the leaders. Norfolk's introduction of the Six Articles as a bill in the English House of Lords, May 1593, was followed by the appearance of the king in person in parliament to urge its passage. The uncompromising orthodoxy of the Six Articles in their insistence upon transubstantiation, private masses and clerical celibacy, was followed by a period of harsh implementation in England.

For Cromwell it was the beginning of the end. Though he retrieved the situation somewhat by the marriage of Henry to Anne, daughter of the Lutheran duke of Cleves, Henry's chagrin at Anne's appearance quickly turned to distaste. Cromwell's blunder led to his rapid downfall. He was executed as a heretic in July 1540 even as Henry procured his divorce from Anne and married Norfolk's niece, Katherine Howard.

It was to Cromwell's party that Dr George Browne belonged both politically and doctrinally. The Six Articles compelled him to step carefully. Cranmer was obliged to send his wife and children to Germany for protection and for the rest of Henry's reign held on to his life precariously. Bishop Shaxton who had opposed the Six Articles in the upper House was imprisoned. Browne who lacked an ideological commitment to the reformation lay low. Cromwell's execution confirmed him in his middle-of-the-road position. Moreover the pro-papal religious campaign whipped up by the Geraldine League in 1539 severely disconcerted the Irish administration in Dublin. Browne realised that he would receive little support from the scared members of the Dublin council if he desired to resume his evangelising activities. In practice however, he lacked the energy of an evangelist. From 1540 onwards a lull in his missionary endeavours ensued.

Pope or king

The deputyship of Lord Leonard Grey had been one of intensive warfare. It was succeeded by the milder period of St Leger in the conviction that the native Irish must be won over by diplomacy and peaceful overtures. The decision to call another parliament which would include representatives of the native Irish was an indication of the new policy. From Henry's point of view the most important bill was that recognising him as king of Ireland. To protect his position and to make it obvious that he was not being elected to the monarchy by this Irish parliament, the bill was redrafted. In it Henry VIII was recognised by the title that was his by inheritance and conquest. It passed without opposition.

Once Chapuys, the astute Spanish ambassador in London had speculated on the consequences of the pope sending an envoy to Ireland and he had concluded 'there would be some commotion for they hold themselves entirely subject to the apostolic see'. Henry VIII held his title now in opposition to the pope and acquiescence in Ireland seemed general. There was one straw in the wind. Early in 1541 Pope Paul III sent a letter to Con O'Neill in answer to one of his. The pope rejoiced to learn that O'Neill considered himself defender of the Roman Church and Catholic religion in Ireland.

3   The beginnings of conquest

The Gaelic lordship in the sixteenth century

The relationship between those who ruled over the native areas of Ireland and the king of England remained ill-defined and tenuous until the reign of Henry VIII. In practice and by status, they were overlords corresponding in prestige to the Anglo-Irish lords but legally, in relation to the king of England no definition of their position had been attempted. The Gaelic overlord ruled over a territory which was referred to, somewhat inaccurately, in sixteenth-century state documents as his 'country'. One of the earliest documents of Henry's reign concerning Ireland, *The State of Ireland and Plan for its Reformation* (1515), indicates official awareness of a 'native problem'.

> 'And first of all to make his Grace understand that there may be more than 60 countries, called regions in Ireland, inhabited with the King's Irish enemies; some regions as big as a shire, some more, some less, unto a little; some as big as half a shire and some a little less; where reigneth more than 60 chief captains ... that liveth only by the sword and obeyeth to no other, temporal persons, but only to himself that is strong . . .'.

The Gaelic lordship was a hidden countryside concealed by natural protective frontiers of woods and by closely guarded passes and fords. Cattle were the symbols of war and wealth. The economic basis of the lordship in the sixteenth century was livestock, and more specifically great herds of cows.

As a region, the Gaelic lordship in the early sixteenth century was as yet recognisably patterned on the structures worked out centuries earlier. In Brehon law, land was held by a class of free landowning families. These Gaelic lords were a nobility whose followers occupied their holdings with a status little higher than that of tenant-at-will in English law, and legally far less precise. The Gaelic lordship was divided into several parts. An area called the *mensal* land belonged to the overlord during his lifetime; it varied in size. Another area was apportioned to the ruling family from which the lord was elected, and the remaining land was allotted to the chief branches of the name. Practice differed. In Munster MacCarthy of Muskerry held nearly half his country as mensal land. In Ulster during the late fifteenth century the overlordship of the O'Neills of Tir Eoghain was challenged by the O'Neills of Clandeboy, who succeeded in making their territory practically independent of the overlord.

Sixteenth-century Ireland was a country where two systems of land tenure operated separately though not in isolation as is clear from the administration of the Desmond Palatinate. The Normans had held their land by feudal tenure as from the king, their liege lord, technically the sole allodial landholder. The holding of land in Gaelic areas was, in general, non-feudal. It was accomplished on two levels, that of *tanistry* which concerned the elective family, and that of *gavelkind* which was a loose arrangement operating between a landholder and his tenants. On the overlord's demesne or mensal land lived his tenants who held land contracts for short periods only. At best they were tenants at will and their contractual obligation to their lord was rather in the form of exchange of cows than in a document or lease of land. Beyond the demesne were the 'freelands' held by the freeholders who gave service of court to their lord, or paid a certain money rent fixed at a standard rate. To the middle of the sixteenth century this rate amounted to ten shillings a ploughland, or a penny an acre. The fiscal unit was the carucate or plough-land but considerable flexibility occurred in Irish land measurements. For instance in Gaelic parts of Munster a 'ploughland' was estimated by an area's capacity to carry cattle, or by the extent of its arable land measured by the number of days it took to plough. In Ulster the ploughland was even more variable. Dr Quinn tentatively calculates that 1,200 ploughlands averaged 300 English acres in the Smith plantation, 1571.

The third division of the Gaelic lordship, equivalent in area to the other two combined, bore the burdens of the lord's impositions. These were 'chargeable lands' con-tributing an uncertain or fluctuating rent if supplies were required for the lord and his household, or for public works, or for defence of the country. When the lord required it, he billeted his fighting men on those lands. In the past this imposition or *buannacht* had not been singularly burdensome since warfare was a seasonal occupation. In the sixteenth century when military conquest became a constant element in English policy, *buannacht* assumed formidable proportions.

The Church lands in Gaelic areas were, in the early sixteenth century, a collection of land holdings consisting of the older monastic settlements administered by the powerful lay administrators, *coarbs* and *erenaghs*, and the newer, continental-type friaries with lands attached like Athenry Dominican friary, endowed by a lord or by a member of the ruling family. Peasant tenants occupied these lands and were bound by ecclesiastical settlement to reside on church lands.

Titles and tenures

One of the important enactments of the Irish Reformation parliament which contemporary events obscured was the Act of Absentees (1537). By it, all lands claimed by the duke of Norfolk, the heirs general of the earls of Ormond and several others including Lord Berkeley, were declared confiscated and vested in the Crown. Though its realisation was impracticable, the Act of Absentees signified that the English monarchy was legal owner of Leinster and Tipperary, as for some centuries it had claimed legal ownership of Ulster and Connaught.[1] In fact the confiscation of properties belonging to the House of Kildare was the only formal confirmation made by Henry VIII in the technical sense but the Act of Absentees introduced a new policy of private negotiations between Henry VIII and the Gaelic lords whose lands lay in regions claimed by absentees, now penalised by the new Act. Lord Leonard Grey was responsible for this new experiment which brought together the Crown and the Irish Lords in a new agreement called 'an indenture'. Grey's efforts to win the Gaelic lords to an acknowledgement of Henry VIII as their king were considerable. Moreover the effectiveness of the indentures in breaking up the Geraldine League was realised by Grey himself. In a report submitted in January 1540 he stated that twenty-seven indentures had been issued and his list included the names of O'Byrne, O'Brian, O'Connor, O'Flaherty, De Burgho, O'Neill, and MacMahon. His success in this field did not save him from trial and subsequent execution for mismanagement of the king's affairs in Ireland.

His successor, St Leger, continued the practice but the character of the indenture changed appreciably in the intervening years. For example, in 1536 O'Byrne promised three guarantees: to be a faithful subject, not to maintain rebels, and to pay certain monies to the king in return for which he was guaranteed possession of his lands and the lord deputy's protection. In September 1540 King Henry authorised St Leger to make grants upon surrender 'to such Irishmen as shall come in and acknowledge their duties towards us' and, a little later, the king dispatched more detailed instructions to his deputy. 'You shall know', he wrote, 'that we divide Irishmen, and the land they occupy, into two parts. The one part as O'Reilly, O'Connor, the Cavanaghs, and c., we take to lie so upon the danger of our power, as you may easily bring them to any reasonable conditions, that may be well desired of them. The other sort, as O'Donnell, McWilliam, O'Brien and c., we think lie so far from our strength there, as, without a greater force, it would be difficult to expel them out of their country . . . we would, that to them all you shall use good and discreet persuasion to make them savour, what it is to have their lands by our gift certainly and quietly . . .'[2] Certainly Manus O'Donnell's terms of agreement in 1541 were more stringent in the guarantees required of him in return for the possession of his lands, and the lord deputy's protection than in earlier indentures. O'Donnell promised to be a faithful subject to the king and not to confederate with rebels. He undertook to renounce the authority of the papacy. He promised to assist the king's hosting in person with his followers, to appear in parliament, to hold his lands from the king with the title given to him by the king. He agreed to carry out the articles contained in the king's letter, and to send one of his sons to England for education.

Evidently the indentures envisaged two groups of Irish lords, those who should be created peers by letters patent, and those who should not. The creation of a peerage from among the native nobility was a daring innovation and the risk of a possible backlash of resentment from the Anglo-Irish lords a considerable one, but the inspiration behind the award of titles derived from another event of some importance, the summoning of another Irish parliament by St Leger.

The 1541 Parliament

A laconic statement published in the *Calendar of State Papers Ireland* under the heading, 26 June 1541 reads: 'Lord

Deputy Sent Leger to the king. "Parliament has met. Act passed for Henry VIII to be king of Ireland." [3]

Parliament met in Dublin. There is a list extant of Irish bishops and peers present in the House of Lords for the passing of the 'Act of the king's style'. Four archbishops, nineteen bishops, and twenty temporal peers participated. Among them were representatives of families long truant in their attendance. Thomas earl of Desmond was in attendance and a number of his satellites such as Fitzmaurice his cousin, and Lords Barry and Roche. Some of the native Irish lords were present or sent representatives. O'Neill of Clandeboy came in person, so did the shrewd Donough O'Brien. MacMurrough, O'More and O'Reilly attended the session though none as yet received titles. The new baron of Upper Ossory, MacGillapatrick, by his presence as baron symbolised the new relationship between Henry VIII and the native aristocracy.

Of the House of Commons we know little. Sir John Davies, addressing the Irish parliament of James I over seventy years later, recalled:

Before the 33rd year of King Henry VIII we do not find any to have place in parliament but the English of blood or English of birth only; for the mere Irish in those days were never admitted, as well because their countries lying out of the limits of counties, could send no knights, and, having neither cities nor boroughs in them, could send no burgesses to the parliament.

The speaker was Sir Thomas Cusack who had advised the king previously on a number of occasions. Both his speech and the reply of the Lord Chancellor were translated into Irish by the earl of Ormond. That same day the 'Act for the King's style' (33 *Henry VIII*, C.I.) was adopted unanimously in both Houses. A Proclamation issued shortly after reflected the general satisfaction of the members – 'to declare our own gladness and joy that his

Majesty is now, as he hath always of right been acknowledged by the Nobility and Commons of this realm of Ireland to be king of the same, and he and his heirs to be named, reputed, and taken for evermore Kings of Ireland.' With such expressions of goodwill one of the most important Acts of an Irish parliament was passed, the work of one day. Some minor Acts were passed, including the confiscation of Lord Leonard Grey's lands, but the other important matter of the 1541 Parliament was the legislation surrounding the exchange of indentures, known as Surrender and Regrant.

Surrender and Regrant

The process known as Surrender and Regrant was first an acknowledgement by the Gaelic lord of the king's authority, then, upon submission, a grant of the territory the lord possessed, and depending on his importance, a title was to be conferred on him. Henceforth Irish and Anglo-Irish were to serve the same monarch in civil and church affairs. They were to speak the same language, hold the same customs, possess their lands in similar fashion. Throughout 1541 the lord deputy received submissions. MacWilliam and MacGillapatrick submitted early in the year, Manus O'Donnell in the autumn and finally Con O'Neill late the following year.

With the acceptance of titles by the Gaelic lords, legal history in Ireland took a new turn. Surrender and Regrant widened the relationship between king and subject to include both native Irish and Anglo-Irish. All were equally entitled to the protection of the law. All were deemed capable of holding land in a precise legal manner in Ireland. The right of access to the king's courts was implicit in the new agreement and the following decades were to witness the extension of English law to all 'free' Irish. A regular system of courts began to function and the justices of the peace assumed a quasi-military role in sixteenth-century

Ireland as the administration of English justice pushed further and deeper into the Gaelic 'countries'. Irish law, so long regarded as native Brehon law, came to mean in the course of successive Tudor reigns, the law applied in the courts in Ireland.

W. F. T. Butler points out that Henry's intention to give legal titles to the actual occupiers of the land was sincere and that he desired to confer a title of lordship valid in English law upon a Gaelic lord and, by that deed, to confirm him in the lordship of the actual keep and demesne lands he occupied.[4] That Henry's covenant with the Gaelic lords had unfortunate results for the other members of the family and for the dependants of the lord will emerge later on. The haste and vagueness with which the documents were worded afforded loopholes to the rapacity both of Crown official and Gaelic lord alike. Increasingly Tudor monarchs, or their officials in Ireland, permitted and even suggested the assumption by the newly-titled lord, of the common property of the family or sept over which he ruled. This was to occur on a large scale in Ulster but a more immediate consequence of Con O'Neill's earldom was the dispute over headship of the family which arose between his sons, Matthew and Shane.

'O'Neil writeth fair letters; howbeit we have no confidence in him', reported Brereton, the lord justice to Henry in July 1540. The new deputy, St Leger, found Con O'Neill elusive and over a year passed in efforts to detach his supporters and subdue him. Con O'Neill's submission eventually took place in December 1541. O'Neill manifested his willingness to attend parliament, to renounce his black rent, to renounce papal authority and to keep the king's peace. He requested the title of earl of Ulster with the same measure of autonomy as Ormond or Desmond. After months of negotiation Henry accepted Con O'Neill as subject to his orders, offering him the title of Tyrone as the earldom of Ulster was considered a royal title. To mark the importance of the occasion O'Neill went to London where his investment took place with a great show of solemnity.

Con O'Neill in assuming the earldom of Tyrone was conferred with the dignity for life together with titles to the manors and lands he possessed up to then as a Gaelic overlord. After his death the earldom was to pass to his son Matthew who was made baron of Dungannon. From him it was to pass to his male heirs for ever. The arrangement flung open to dispute the long-held dynastic claims of the O'Neills to elect their overlord. More immediately, it brought into the open the rivalry between Matthew and Shane, the two sons of Con. Matthew's legitimacy and paternity were both challenged by Shane. Nevertheless Matthew O'Neill was accepted by the deputy as the most important of O'Neill's sons in 1541. Almost a generation older than Shane – a mere boy at that time – Matthew was evidently regarded by the ageing Con as his *tanaist*, though in fact Con's nephew, Niall Connalach, and Niall's son Turlough Luineach, were both in a position to make a stronger bid for *tanaist* than Matthew. Whether or not St Leger and his council connived at placing Matthew in the coveted position of heir apparent is open to debate but the result of Con's acceptance of earldom was a divided Ulster of internal conflicts. Short-lived alliances and deep feuds emerged as the different branches of the O'Neill family grappled with the inexorable consequences of exchanging the honours of the *derbfine* for the more tangible ones of titled aristocracy.

The years of stock-taking

The succession act of 1543 secured the Crown for the Tudors by arranging that Edward and then Mary and Elizabeth would succeed their father in that order. It was to prove a critical decade and the crisis did not pass away with Elizabeth's accession in 1558. King Henry's final years were burdened by debt, the consequences of a debased coinage already manifesting themselves in the economy. Vast tracts of crown lands despoiled from the monasteries were sold or alienated recklessly after the execution of Thomas Cromwell, that careful steward. The invasion of France and the holding of Boulogne by the English proved expensive and in the end, a trivial episode. Henry's death at the age of fifty-seven placed his nine year old son on the throne. Though Henry had anticipated dissent by appointing a council, that council immediately appointed Edward's uncle, the duke of Somerset, protector of the realm.

The reigns of Edward VI (1547–53) and of his sister Mary (1553–58) brought to the surface the tensions of social unrest and religious disharmony which were everywhere rising in various parts of Europe. Somerset's protectorship ushered in official Protestantism and despite a Catholic reaction in the reign of Mary, the country adhered to the Anglican settlement which Elizabeth I offered as a compromise.

Edward Seymour, Duke of Somerset, faced one crisis after another during his three years as Lord Protector. In Norfolk, Kett's rising in 1549 was followed by a Catholic rising of the peasantry in the west. The risings were crushed, John Dudley, Earl of Warwick being prominent in carrying out the executions that followed. Warwick, taking advantage of the general desire for order, posed as the saviour of the kingdom, adroitly discrediting Somerset in the process. The latter's untimely death in 1552 paved the way for the rule of Dudley, now Earl of Northumberland. His hard-line Protestant policy consolidated the English reformation but he overreached himself in his ambitious schemes for his family. His sponsoring of Lady Jane Grey, his daughter-in-law, as the successor to the dying Edward met with widespread resistance and Mary Tudor was proclaimed queen of England on a surge of popular loyalty to the Tudors.

In Ireland the last years of Henry's reign were stewarded by Sir Anthony St Leger. As deputy he was to serve on three occasions and he proved a fair-minded administrator, earning from Campion the praise: 'a discreet gentleman, very studious of the state of Ireland, enriched, stout enough, without gall.

St Leger had been one of the original 1537 commissioners appointed by Henry to draw up a report on the state of Ireland and to enquire into the behaviour of Lord Deputy Grey. He brought to his appointment as lord deputy an understanding of his role and a remarkable grasp of the necessity of winning the friendship of the native Irish lords. He was conservative in his rule of Ireland but he was also an innovator. With his deputyship constitutional trends in the governing of Ireland, perceptible since the previous decade, became more obvious. St Leger realised that Grey's continual warfare had drained the country. An energetic campaign in the territories surrounding the Pale, reduced the O'Tooles and the O'Connors to submission and eventual co-operation. In his advice to Henry VIII and his privy councillors he proposed the exchange of title and the holding of land by knight's service in the case of O'Toole and later in those of O'Connor, O'Donnell and O'Neill.

Leinster enjoyed a degree of tranquillity under the first deputyship of St Leger which the province had not experienced for over two decades. He summoned a parliament, successfully got the king's legislation through and found time to draw up a 'Device for Reformation of Leinster' which Henry subsequently rejected. English law was extended outwards from the Pale and the rough outlines of a new county, that of Westmeath, were drawn. Sheriffs were appointed in Wicklow. By 1547 no other Englishman had such an intuitive grasp of Irish affairs and no Englishman of his time was as universally esteemed in Ireland as Anthony St Leger.

Yet he encountered hostility of the concealed type which was a permanent feature of the administration in Dublin. Piers Butler had resumed the Ormond title in 1538 and passed it on to his son, James, the following year, together with the first of the monastic properties with which the Butler lordship was to be augmented in the next few decades. James Butler was an energetic soldier, a loyal adherent of Henry VIII and a professional complaint-carrier. With Alen, the new chancellor, he now constituted the chief opposition to St Leger and charged the lord deputy with 'erecting a Geraldine band'.

St Leger, after a brief visit to England, returned to find Ormond plotting with other factious spirits, – the new earl of Desmond being one of them, – O'More and O'Carroll of Ely. St Leger prudently decided to return to England to defend himself against the charges of Ormond and Alen. Accusations of maladministration were brought against him. In particular it was alleged that he allowed the Irish enemies to muster strength and that his favouring of O'Connor was inimical to the interests of the Crown.

St Leger denied all charges. He was supported by testimonies from Ireland. A number of lords of diverse backgrounds, the lords of Tyrone, Thomond, the barons of Upper Ossory, O'Connor, O'Carroll of Ely, even Desmond, addressed a memorial to Henry protesting that the charges were unfounded and that the deputy had protected well the king's interests. A unique tribute to St Leger, they requested King Henry that if St Leger was not to return, a deputy of a like nature be sent in his place. St Leger worked hard for his vindication which was a personal triumph. Chancellor Alen was removed from office and James earl of Ormond died mysteriously in London before the year was out. St Leger returned to Ireland secure in his deputyship and was retained in office by the Protector, Somerset, after Henry's death.

The second return of St Leger as deputy was brief and contemporary documents afford few glimpses of his personal administration. In his absence power had passed into the hands of the vice-treasurer, Sir William Brabazon who proceeded to goad the lord of Offaly, Brian O'Connor, into rebellion. In a short time mid-Leinster was once more in arms. This time Leix and Offaly were to pay the full reckoning.

Leix and Offaly at the accession of Henry VIII was territory anciently held by the O'Mores and the O'Connors, subsequently granted to the Normans and in the following centuries again won back by the O'Mores, O'Connors, and by the sub-chieftains, the O'Dunnes of Iregan, and the O'Carrolls of Ely. The O'Connors of Offaly had grown powerful and by the beginning of the sixteenth century menaced the Pale along the borders of Kildare and Meath. Their first Tudor rebellion on a large scale broke out in 1520 on Surrey's arrival and after a series of skirmishes, an inconclusive submission was tendered by O'Connor to Surrey. It was a decade in which sympathy for the Geraldines waxed and waned but Brian O'Connor, Lord of Offaly, adhered steadfastly to Garret Fitzgerald, bound by ties of kinship and fealty. On one occasion he took the vice-deputy, Baron Delvin, prisoner and let it be known that 'within a year the king he hoped would have no further jurisdiction in Ireland'. Yet in 1530 he allowed himself to be persuaded by Alice, his sister-in-law, daughter of the earl of Kildare, to make peace and he submitted. An uneasy truce prevailed.

The rebellion of Silken Thomas roused the lords of Leix and Offaly into war once more. It was a war of attrition with allies melting away by degrees until O'Connor alone held out. His capitulation to Skeffington and to the newly-arrived Grey completed the first phase of the Geraldine downfall. In Cowley's shrewd estimation, O'Connor had to be destroyed since Offaly was so close to the Pale that it would eventually extend to encompass it, he predicted. Alen, then Master of the Rolls, went further and sketched the first outlines of the future plantation. There was only one way, he said, to ensure permanent subjugation of that region and that was to banish the natives, including the O'Connors, and plant the territory with loyal subjects in their place.

In 1537 Grey took the field against Brian O'Connor and in a classic pincerlike move, isolated him, at the same time creating Brian's brother, Cahir O'Connor, lord of Offaly. Grey too recommended the planting of a colony of Englishmen and the award of an English title to the new lord of Offaly. However Brian O'Connor retrieved an almost hopeless situation in a masterly recoupment, winning the admiration of both Grey and St Leger. St Leger then a commissioner in Ireland commented:

> that same country is much easier won than kept for, unless it be peopled with other than be there already and also certain fortresses builded and warded, if it be gotten the one day, it is lost the next.

Brian O'Connor finally tendered his submission to Grey who travelled into Offaly to receive it. It was ratified in Dublin shortly afterwards. The terms of the indenture were severe but O'Connor seemed anxious for English tenure and for a title. These Grey promised. The respite brought two years of prosperity to Offaly and Grey's enemies witnessed with dislike the growing friendship between Brian O'Connor and the deputy. One of the charges brought against Grey at his trial was that he surrounded himself with former rebels against the Crown.

The recall of Lord Leonard Grey and his subsequent arrest was the signal for a fresh outburst of raids upon the Pale by Brian O'Connor. He had not yet received the desired baronetcy and, as on previous occasions, he tendered his submission when he deemed fit. His timing was well-calculated. The new deputy Sir Anthony St Leger was disposed to plead his cause with Henry and worded a vigorous plea for mercy to the king:

'If O'Connor's petition was granted, he would give good service, or else the respite could afford time to cut passes and build fortresses which O'Connor had agreed to facilitate.' The king acquiesed but the request for English tenure by Brian O'Connor was set aside. It was still a vague promise four years later when St Leger departed for England in circumstances that recalled his pre-decessor. Once again Henry's deputy had to defend himself against the charges of Ormond and Alen.

Deprived of St Leger's friendly presence and unaware that the deputy was even then in the presence of the English Privy Council accusing Lord Chancellor Alen of malice against the lord of Offaly, Brian O'Connor together with Gillapatrick O'More, lord of Leix, broke out in rebellion against Brabazon. The rebellion was regarded as serious enough to warrant a report on it, sent from London to the king of France in November 1546. In view of the international situation it was a serious rebellion. King Henry VIII was dying. The Desmond Geraldines were turbulent in Munster and were again seeking a continental alliance, this time with France and Scotland.

The lords-in-rebellion were proclaimed traitors and their lands were declared confiscated to the Crown. Brabazon, now lord justice, pushed further into Offaly, trying to establish an English foothold in the territory. Neither the death of Henry VIII nor the re-appointment of St Leger six months later brought any slackening in Brabazon's determination to exterminate the lords of Leix and Offaly. Though St Leger received back his appointment as deputy, the management of the war was entrusted to Captain Bellingham, an experienced soldier. The replacement as deputy of the mild, conservative St Leger by the energetic soldier was confirmed the following year, 1548. More than anything Bellingham's appointment as deputy signified the determination to speed on the process of confiscation by conquest. Bellingham was the first lord deputy for over two hundred years to extend the Pale.

The beginnings of extension

Morrin in his Preface to the *Calendar of Patent Rolls of Ireland* points out that Bellingham extended the Pale by the sword. His strategy was similar to 'the method of the frontiers' in the newly-discovered territories of North America. After a rapid and ruthless campaign, he began the construction of military roads into Offaly and Leix, paying particular attention to the widening of 'passes' and the building of a fortress which he superintended from Athy within the Pale. In a short time the new fortress, called in the beginning Fort Protector (after Somerset), later Maryborough in honour of Queen Mary Tudor, began to take shape as another outpost of the Pale. Daingean in Offaly was chosen as a second outpost, becoming known as Philipstown in due course. As for the lords of Leix and Offaly they were escorted to London by St Leger where they received free pardons and exile. The more bellicose of their followers were enlisted for the king's service and shipped to France, so ridding the new deputy of an un-welcome intrusion upon his work. Leighlin Bridge, the passage out of the Pale to the south was further strengthened as a garrison, and the acquisition of the Carmelite Monastery there as a new fortress served to emphasise the changes that had taken place within a decade. By the spring of 1549 most of the baronies of Meath and Westmeath were cessed for building and fortifying in Offaly. The way was open for colonisation.

There is no substantial body of evidence to indicate that a whole-scale plantation of Leix and Offaly was contemplated at this period. The fears that the Gaelic areas of Ireland would form alliances with the Scots and the French or with other European powers were capable of realisation at any point during the next half-century. The plantation of Leix and Offaly evolved from various experiments to build up a 'frontier' colony under government auspices. In June 1550 the English Privy Council 'agreed upon diverse good considerations, that Leix and Offaly, being the countries late O'Connors and O'Mores, should be let out to the King's subjects at convenient rents, to the intent it may both be inhabited and also a more strength for the King's Majesty'.

St Leger, though unwillingly, was once again appointed lord deputy in July 1550. He proceeded to initiate the plantation somewhat reluctantly. Walter Cowley undertook the task of surveying the territories, a task he accomplished with haste and inexperience as was subsequently discovered. Already a small clique, Anglo-Irish by birth, government official by profession offered to undertake the new plantation. Among the petitioners were Sir Gerald Aylmer, chief justice of the King's Bench, Sir Thomas Luttrell, chief justice of the common pleas, Sir John Travers, master of the ordinances and Patrick Barnewall, master of the rolls. Their offer which found favour with St Leger because it left some lands among the original occupiers, was rejected by the English Privy Council. The latter preferred to lease tracts of land to certain English gentlemen and to soldiers who had helped to suppress the late rebellion.

The appointment of Sir James Crofts to succeed St Leger as deputy marked a significant stage in the plantation schemes. Crofts went ahead with the surveying and strongly urged the setting up of legal machinery to reduce the territories of Leix and Offaly to English acreage. Manors should be erected and the land leased by copyhold tenures. Fresh outbursts of rebellion and resistance on the part of the original occupiers of the lands forced him to reconsider his views. Thieves plundered the settler country driving off cattle and rendering it almost uninhabitable. The return of Brian O'Connor and Gerald, earl of Kildare on free pardon by Queen Mary added fuel to the resistance. 'There was great rejoicing throughout the greater part of Leath-Mhogha because of their arrival; for it was thought that not one of the descendants of the earls of Kildare, or of O'Connor Fahy, would ever come to Ireland', reported the *Annals of the Four Masters*. The reappointment of St Leger as deputy coincided with the return of Brian O'Connor, but for the most part, St Leger was occupied with Ulster where trouble had been brewing among the O'Neills. An uneasy state of affairs was ended by the appointment of Sir Thomas Ratcliffe, later known as the earl of Sussex, as deputy in April 1556.

The plantation gets under way

The explicit directions issued to Ratcliffe together with the legislation passed in the Irish parliament the following year formed the model of colonisation procedure for the plantations which were to follow. Surveying, selection of settlers, arrangement of land tenures by fee-farm, and finally parliamentary legislation were the main administrative steps in the strategy of plantation. Ratcliffe was instructed to begin by erecting the territories into the status of new counties.

> Touching the said countries our special intent and desire is, that the same and the rest of our whole realm, should by authority of Parliament be made shire ground and divided into sufficient and reasonable counties as our realm of England is; that the said countries should be also divided into townships, manors and baronies, as our counties of Meath, Kildare, Kilkenny and other are; and into parishes if the same have churches, convenient and necessary lying for the same.

Even more arresting were the conditions of land leasing in the newly-erected shires. Settlers were required to hold their land in tail male specifying an annual rent per acre. A settler was to maintain a number of armed retainers and he was obliged to attend with his tenants armed and provisioned for three days. He was also to set aside for the constable of the Maryborough or Philipstown fortress – depending on where he lived – one ploughday for each plough on his lands. Alternatively he agreed to carry out such work as the constable of the fortress would allocate. Once a year he was to appear before the constable or sheriff of the county with the men under his jurisdiction capable of bearing arms between the ages of sixteen and sixty. Further he was to go guarantee for their good conduct. He agreed to keep open or closed the fords in his lands as directed by the constable and, if the deputy or his representative thought fit, he must submit to the alteration of water courses on his lands, and to allow wood to be taken for the building purposes of the country.

It was then a military tenancy that was being offered. Planters were not allowed to maintain men of Irish blood born outside the county and experienced in arms, nor could they marry or have any dealings with Irish men and women who lived outside the shires of the kingdom. They could not exact coyne or livery to be levied on them, nor could they assist or in any manner hire themselves out for illegal raids.

Ratcliffe assigned 'all the country beyond the bog' west of Maryborough to the O'Mores. The O'Connors were apportioned land west of Daingean. The head of each of the families was to become a landlord holding his lands in tail male under similar conditions to those of the settlers. He could not keep 'idlemen' and he was to attend the constable when required, to repair bridges, to keep the passes open between the English and the Gaelic districts. He was to adopt the English style of dress, to teach his children to speak the English language, and to attend the deputy annually. He was to employ solely common law; settlers were forbidden to resort to Brehon Law. Marrying and fostering with the neighbouring Irish was a penalty.

Parliament was summoned for June 1557. Ratcliffe, who was rewarded for his labours with the earldom of Sussex, was responsible for its convening and for accomplishing its main legislation, the Acts known as 3rd and 4th Philip and Mary:

> Be it therefore ordained, enacted and established . . . that the said King's and Queen's Majesties . . . shall have, hold and possess for ever, as in the right of the Crown of England and Ireland, the said countries of Leix, Slewmarge, Irry, Glinmaliry and Offaly . . . and to the end the said countries may be from henceforth the better conserved, and kept in civil government; be it enacted . . . that the new fort in Leix, be from henceforth for ever called and named Maryborough, and that the said countries . . . as standeth and is situate on that side of the river of Barrow, whereupon the said Maryborough standeth and is situated . . . be from the first day of this Parliament, one shire or county named the Queen's County shall from the said day be taken, reputed, and used as a county and there shall be appointed, ordained and made within the said shire or county, for the rule thereof . . . sheriffs, coroners, escheator, clerk of the market etc.

As W. F. T. Butler points out in connection with the Munster Plantation, the rebellion of a chieftain henceforth incurred grave penalties in law. Though more clearly seen in Munster on the death of the earl of Desmond in 1583, the legislation of the Leix and Offaly plantation (Acts 3, 4, Philip and Mary) based the Crown's claim to the lands upon the continued rebellion of the natives against royal authority. Leix and Offaly were confiscated to the Crown by attainder of their owners following their rebellion against the Crown. It was stated that they had 'usurped' the Crown's possession of the lands. Moreover Edward VI was cited as the original claimant and no reference was made to any prior claim such as the older feudal claim to the one-time Mortimer escheated lands. To Sussex was reserved the right of granting estates and, in that manner, of selecting the settlers. As for the O'Mores and O'Connors, they were not considered to be included in the clause 'all and every their majesties subject, English or Irish, born within this realm or within the realm of England'.

Sussex combined to a remarkable degree the virtues of the new Elizabethan official. A soldier and seasoned campaigner, he was a first-class administrator. Between 1556 and 1563 he journeyed systematically through Ireland. He saw and recorded the limitations of local administration. The shiring of the whole country he regarded as central to any administrative system because only through the establishment of shire officials could English common law function. The revival of the office of sheriff whose office in Tudor Ireland was an important one in the new bureaucracy was a figure whom St Leger and Sussex both regarded as the real keeper of law and order. More commanding than the constable whose authority was force, more permanent than a lieutenant whose office was also military, the justice of the peace brought civic order to a locality.

Yet it was to a lieutenant that the two new shires were entrusted. Sir Henry Ratcliffe, brother of Sussex, was entrusted with the care of the new plantations. Originally it was planned to have 160 English settlers. By 1563 a new survey had been completed to replace the botched Cowley one and the boundary commissioners completed their report. Though records no longer exist, there would seem to have been not less than eighty grants and the grantees were divided into three classes: gentlemen of the Pale, officers and soldiers of the army, and native Irish of the territories. Estates ranged in size from 3,302 acres to twenty-five acres. Among the gentlemen of the Pale who received land were Henry Cowley, the baron of Delvin, Richard Pepper, Sir Thomas Tyrell, and the earl of Ormond. The latter received 820 acres including the monastic lands of Abbeyleix. The officers and soldiers who had campaigned in the Leix-Offaly rebellions were amply rewarded. Robert Harpole, the constable of Carlow Castle received 553 acres. Captain Henry Brereton received 537 acres; Captain Henry Warren 620 acres.

But it was among the native Irish that the largest grants were allocated. Owen MacHugh O'Dempsey who had killed Donough O'Connor the most formidable of the O'Connors after Brian was rewarded with what corresponded to the one-time *tuath* or barony of Clanmaliere, a barony in size amounting to 3,302 acres. The cultivation of 'loyal' Irish was to be a minor but important feature of subsequent plantations.

The plantation of Leix and Offaly remained for over forty years a problem to the administration in Dublin and to the Tudor monarch who best understood the necessity for colonisation, Queen Elizabeth. It was she who instructed her deputy, Sidney, to pacify the native inhabitants of Leix and Offaly by a general pardon after one of their uprisings in 1565 but she further directed that the courts be extended to adjoining Irish districts, and that sheriffs be appointed for the new counties. Significantly she recommended that the Irish regions between the Shannon and the Pale be annexed to the adjoining counties of King's and Queen's Counties, to Meath and Westmeath.

Elizabeth I was to learn from experience what Sir Anthony St Leger had noted in his report on the activities of the O'Connors and the O'Neills twenty years earlier: Leix and Offaly were 'much easier won than kept'. A contemporary description for the 1570s supplies the text:

out of these wastes, as out of the fortress, in small
companies or great, as occasion requireth or as the turn
is best served, the rebels issueth into the heart of the
Queen's county and thence into every part of the Pale
adjoining, spoiling the same at pleasure . . .

Intractable, unsubdued the O'Connors and O'Mores
continued to harass the government until Deputy
Chichester, working under the experienced James I, late
come from similar problems in Scotland with his highlanders, devised the notion of transplantation.

D. B. Quinn has pointed out in an important study, that
Ireland was 'a unique example of a territory which was
colonised in the twelfth and thirteenth centuries in a feudal
setting and which was recolonised in the sixteenth and
seventeenth centuries in a post-feudal setting'.[5] Tudor
policy throughout this century was one of conciliation on
one level, and of a developing objective to extend the
conquest throughout the whole country. The first policy,
that of pacifying the Gaelic and Anglo-Irish lords was
more congenial to the Tudor monarchy; the second,
harsher, more ruthless was applied only in particular
instances. It was this latter policy which underlaid sixteenth-century colonisation experiments. By the middle of
the century factors had appeared which made the reality of
plantation certain. The government required permanent
garrisons to inhabit the conquered areas near the Pale and
it was gradually realised that a permanent plantation of
English settlers around a central defence core was probably
the cheapest and most stable means of accomplishing this
strategy. Bellingham, St Leger and Crofts had begun by
placing garrisons as shields along the eastern frontier of the
Pale in the Gaelic areas of Leix and Offaly. Under Sussex
this developed into an impressive attempt to build up the
classic frontier colony under government auspices. The
chief concern was a military one. Little attention was paid
to problems of society.

4 Elizabethan Ireland

Progress of the Reformation

The death of Henry VIII ostensibly removed the most formidable obstacle to the progress of the reformation in England, the person of the king. The rejection of papal jurisdiction had signified the abandoning of those church doctrines on which papal supremacy was founded, but until the death of Henry VIII the divergence between Rome and the English monarch was primarily over jurisdiction and the Henrician Church was a church in schism. With the reign of Edward VI came the public acknowledgement of the liturgical and theological dimensions of the English Reformation.

Somerset, as Lord Protector, retained complete control of the government for three years, and under his moderate rule the English reformation progressed. Parliament abolished the worst features of the Treasons Act, repealed the Act of the Six Articles, and pushed ahead with the 1545 law on the dissolution of chantries. Communion in both kinds and marriage of the clergy were legalised. Cranmer's *Book of Common Prayer* was declared obligatory as the official form of service and the English parliament passed the first Act of Uniformity in 1549 imposing upon all churches Cranmer's form of service.

Somerset's downfall was followed by the rule of Northumberland. Repressive and uncompromising, Northumberland attempted to suppress all heterodox opinions. He pursued a rigorous church policy which showed influences of both Lutheranism and Calvinism. One of his aims was to exclude Mary's claims to the throne by making England sufficiently Protestant to do so. That effort and his appropriation of confiscated church wealth for himself and his friends prepared the way for a Catholic reaction under Mary Tudor, despite the fact that in 1554 Mary had married the future King Philip II, son of the Emperor Charles V.

In Ireland the progress of the reformation did not parallel that of England. Distance, slowness of communication, the composition of the Dublin administration and the personalities of the chief reformers caused the reformation to suffer a distinct sea-change between London and Dublin. For one thing the reformation bishops in Ireland acted in response to Crown policy and their zeal lay in service to the Crown rather than in a desire to put across the new reformation theology. While Henry VIII succeeded in augmenting royal control over ecclesiastical matters in Ireland he caused no alarm in those parts of Ireland still autonomous. The Protectorate, however, envisaged a religious policy which would impose uniformity on England and Ireland irrespective of local conditions.

The picture of the Edwardian reformation in Ireland does not emerge clearly. The pursuance of a coercive church policy in conjunction with a plantation scheme of a repressive nature caused confusion among English officials in Ireland and makes it difficult to chart the progress of the reformation in the 1550s.

One reason for the obscurity lies in the nature of the documentary source material of this period. The interpolations of Robert Ware, a religious controversialist writing over a hundred years later, produced a mass of skilful forgeries within the collections and writings of his father, the seventeenth-century antiquarian, Sir James Ware. The history of the early reformation in Ireland was a special target of Robert Ware's faked documents and until the historian Philip Wilson in this century systematically examined the writings of Sir James Ware, the 1550s continued to trap the unsuspecting historian who consulted the Ware collections.[1] Yet another contributing factor towards the obscurity of this period lies in the absence of state papers for the middle years of this decade. The preservation of documents in the sixteenth century was, in the main, haphazard; often state papers were at the disposal of a lord deputy or members of a privy council.

The first months of Edward VI's reign passed peacefully in Ireland under the government of Deputy St Leger. With his recall in April 1548, Bellingham was appointed and the introduction of the Edwardian reformation into Ireland became a reality. The first intimations came from Bellingham himself who insisted on adherence to the king's *Injunctions*. The *Order of Communion* followed and with it the endeavour to suppress the Catholic Mass.

It was the introduction of the liturgy, not doctrinal issues, which wrought division among the bishops in Ireland. Archbishop Browne was clearly not at ease. Unhappily caught between his wishes to adhere to government policy and the rapidity with which official reformation policy in Ireland became subordinated to the desire not to provoke either rebellion or foreign invasion, Archbishop Browne found himself in the autumn of 1548 shoring up Somerset's order forbidding preachers to introduce controversial matters into their sermons at a time when official policy in England was playing down any extreme manifestations of religious repression. In 1549 Browne introduced the *Book of Common Prayer* in the Dublin diocese and for the next year and a half busied himself with removing the stone altars from churches in his diocese, among others that of Christ Church cathedral. Perhaps he realised that his earlier action against Preacher Walter the Scot had given the impression that he supported the orthodox Mass of the Henrician reformation, at any rate his tardiness in adopting the liturgy of the second *Book of Common Prayer* in 1552 brought him into active collision with John Bale, the ex-Carmelite, whom Browne consecrated bishop of Ossory in that year. John Bale, far more committed than Browne in his doctrinal position, proceeded to impose the new liturgy on his diocese but relates his failure in his book, *Vocacyon of John Bale*: 'helpers I found none amonge my prebendaries and clergie, but adversaries a great nombre.'

The publication and issue in Ireland of the new rite connected with the *Book of Common Prayer* had the effect of establishing a second liturgy in the country, one that was to be increasingly associated with the colonisation schemes. Significantly Primate Dowdall rejected the new liturgy, declaring to his cousin, Sir Thomas Cusack that 'he wolde never be bishope: where Holie Masse . . . was abolished'. Subsequently he left the country and remained an exile until recalled by Queen Mary.

The reign of Queen Mary

The fires of Smithfield which entered deeply into the folk-memory of England had no counterpart in Ireland. Her reign inaugurated the era of plantations by establishing Leix and Offaly as planted shires but the restoration of the old religion took place without harshness. The clergy of Kilkenny in Bishop Bale's diocese were a barometer of popular attitudes. They restored without official sanction the old sacramentals and shortly afterwards Bishop Bale left his diocese never to return. Archbishop Browne reverted to Catholic practice but because he was married lost the See of Dublin. Primate Dowdall returned to Armagh from his self-imposed exile.

It was however the old religion of Henry VIII. Queen Mary's English parliament had refused to rescind the Royal Supremacy and Mary continued to write '&C' after her secular titles. She also was vigilant in maintaining her right of nomination of bishops though after her formal reconciliation with the Holy See she did not appoint to ecclesiastical sees. Under the influence of Cardinal Pole her adviser, Mary as monarch of England was reconciled formally with Rome and in response to Mary's petition Pole requested the papacy to erect Ireland into a kingdom, a request granted by Paul IV in June 1555.

It was during Mary's reign that Ireland began to experience the politics of religion. Protestantism was reversible. The mission of Primate Robert Wauchop as papal envoy to assess the weakness of the Reformation among the territories of the Northern princes in 1550 was a straw in the wind. The nomination of Cardinal Pole as papal legate to Ireland in July 1555 was a more ostensible indication that the papacy was prepared to stake its claim for retention of Ireland's loyalty to the Holy See. Finally the plantation of Leix and Offaly became inextricably bound up with the Elizabethan Church Settlement. Henceforth *Hibernia Anglicana* would be associated with the Anglican Church.

The Elizabethan Church Settlement

Elizabeth ascended the throne of England at the age of twenty-five. In her long reign of forty-five years she exemplified the solitariness of authority. 'She seems to me', reported Feria, the Spanish ambassador, 'incomparably more feared than her sister, and gives her orders and has her way absolutely, as her father did.'

At her accession the Anglican Church she supported was vague in definition, calvanist in theology, Catholic in structure. Even before parliament met in England, the first weeks of her reign indicated Elizabeth's inclination for a state church of which, by virtue of being sovereign, she was Head. There was the incident on Christmas Day when she commanded Bishop Oglethorpe to omit the elevation of the host at Mass, and her withdrawal on his refusal to comply, an action repeated shortly afterwards at her

Coronation Service. At the state opening of parliament she ordered the monks of Westminster to extinguish their ceremonial tapers and she selected Dr Richard Cox, her brother's tutor and a zealous member of the Prayer Book commissions to preach on that occasion. Parliament met with a well-organised and vigorous Commons and a House of Lords subservient mainly to the monarch's wishes. The Church Settlement which was hammered out was a compromise between the forces of Protestant progressives in the Commons and more moderate elements in the House of Lords who generally acted in concert with the government. From the first Elizabeth had shown she intended to reign as a Protestant monarch and Parliament defined her legal authority over the Church with the Acts of Supremacy and Uniformity. The gradual consolidation of the Anglican Church was one of the achievements of the Elizabethan age but the attainment of an equilibrium between Protestant and Catholic ideals was a much slower and more painful process for the English people. From the beginning, Elizabeth had two oppositions to deal with: Puritans and Catholics, and it was under the banner of religion that political opposition to Elizabeth's government found expression in England and in Ireland.

According to Feria, the Spanish ambassador, there was expressed dissatisfaction about the intended Reform policy among Irishmen with whom he was in touch. It was even mooted that a confederation of Irish lords was being formed to resist the changes. Mary's lord deputy, the earl of Sussex, was again appointed by Elizabeth and was instructed to convene parliament, bringing Ireland into line with England by similar legislation.

The Irish Parliament which met in Dublin in January 1560 was intended to be a rubber-stamp. Though precautions were taken to control the members and ensure compliance, the scanty evidence available points to a strong opposition. Of the internal workings of Elizabeth's first Irish parliament nothing is known, but the personnel of the lower House indicates a large Catholic majority. Yet according to the statute-roll, this parliament enacted the series of Acts which legislated for the Elizabethan church settlement on the lines enacted by the English Parliament, and re-established the Anglican Church in Ireland.

How the Catholic opposition was disposed of is a matter of conjecture among historians. Philip Wilson is of the opinion that the Dublin Parliament was dissolved on the defeat of the measures, and after the sudden departure of Sussex to London by order of the queen, they appeared on the statute-roll and were, in fact, the rejected bills. Professor Jourdan states that with Convocation of the clergy which took place simultaneously with the opening of Parliament, 'the oath of supremacy became a practical thing'. Dr R. D. Edwards points out that fifty years later a group of Catholic petitioners to King James I alleged that the Acts of the 1560 Parliament were manoeuvered onto the statute-roll by a trick and that the belief existed among the Old English of the Pale that the laws were put through on a day when the majority had been told there would be no business. 'But in whatever way it reached the statute-roll, it is necessary to consider the provisions of this legislation, since it was regarded as law in Ireland', concludes Dr Edwards.[2]

The Elizabethan Church Settlement in Ireland restored royal supremacy over the Church on the lines laid down in England. Accompanying it was a new Oath of Supremacy imposed on all ecclesiastical persons, on office-holders, judges, mayors, holders of sinecures hereditary or otherwise, members of universities, minors-at-law; in short it was all-embracing. Furthermore there were severe penalties for abstention from the oath: lifelong incapacity to hold office, loss of property, heavy fines. Next came an Act of Uniformity of Common Prayer which prescribed the form of prayer and religious rites to be used throughout the kingdom, the Edwardian 1552 *Book of Common Prayer* being nominated. It, too, was accomplished by penalties and fines for non-observance, and applied as stringently to the laity as it did to the clergy. To render its implementation more efficient, ecclesiastical officers were entitled to co-operate with civil officers in ensuring its enforcement. The election of bishops and archbishops was to be abolished, the queen having the right to nominate to and fill vacancies. Other acts restored first fruits to the Crown and recognised the queen's title to the throne and her legitimacy.

The ecclesiastical legislation of Henry VIII's reign was the core of the church law re-established by Elizabeth. Her first Irish parliament reversed Mary's ecclesiastical legislation, and drew upon that of her father, adding to it an Act of Uniformity on the lines of that legislated in England in 1559. These Acts together with a select body of laws culled from past Irish parliaments and with additional legislation from the 1569 Irish parliament formed the *corpus* of the first collection of Irish statutes printed in 1572. It had taken thirty years to carry into effect a proposal to collect and print the principal Irish statutes. They were formally published in London in 1572 due largely to the persever-ance of Sir Henry Sidney, Cecil, and James Stanihurst, Speaker in 1569–70 of the Irish House of Commons. Copies for official use were immediately circulated and became the pillar of judicial orthodoxy in Ireland. Dr D. B. Quinn suggests that every copy over the next fifty years 'was systematically employed by officials until it was worn out . . . thus the collection proved a most valuable instrument in the hands of the anglicising officials during the crucial period between 1572–1620 when English law was being painfully imposed on Irish and Anglo-Irish areas alike'![3] As we shall see in a later chapter the Elizabethan Church Settlement became the foundation of a state penal code inextricably bound up with a policy of colonialism. It may be argued that the evangelising features of the Elizabethan Settlement were resisted because of the overtones of colonial repression.

Elizabeth, Sidney and Shane O'Neill

Government to be efficient must be informed. To what extent was Queen Elizabeth informed about Irish matters? The second half of the sixteenth century is rich in documentation ranging from the official state papers inscribed Eliz. R. to the literary evidence of English observers like Campion or Barnaby Rich and the highly allusive bardic satires written in Irish. Throughout her reign Elizabeth carried on a personal correspondence on Irish matters and her letters to Sidney reveal the characteristics of her relationship with Ireland as few other documents do. Sidney is continually scolded about his procrastination. Elizabeth never admits that her troops or the money she allots to Ireland may not be sufficient, yet as her biographer Sir John Neale brings out, she possessed to a high degree the ability to convey her realisation of the pleasure received in serving her, even as she administered a rebuke.

Elizabeth sent some of her ablest and most talented servants to Ireland. She retained in office Mary's lord deputy, the Earl of Sussex but shortly after her accession she elevated him to the position of lord lieutenant, appointing Henry Sidney lord deputy. Sidney came to be regarded as the best colonial administrator of his time. Sir John Perrot, Sir Peter Carew and his brother George saw service in Ireland. Elizabeth sent her two favourites, the senior Essex in the 1570s and the ill-fated son in 1599. Mountjoy, the greatest English soldier of the period, was sent to fight against Hugh O'Neill. The Norris brothers, Sir Richard Bingham, Henry Bagenal, Sir William Pelham – Elizabeth's reign in Ireland is a roll-call of the best of Elizabethan soldiers. Ireland drew English philosophers and poets: Barnaby Rich, Geoffrey Fenton and Sir John Davies; Spenser, Sir Walter Raleigh, Edmund Campion. The colonial projects in Ireland of Sir Thomas Smith, Sir Humphrey Gilbert, Sir Richard Grenville and Sir Walter Raleigh turned the attention of Elizabethan adventurers towards North America.

Sussex was a key figure in implementing Elizabeth's policy in Ireland. In the middle years of her reign he was the only one of that inner circle in the Privy Council who had served in Ireland. His correspondence from Ireland to her is voluminous, his knowledge perceptive, his suggestions full of keen insights. How large a part Sussex's recommendations to Elizabeth played in determining her love of action may be gauged by the amount of latitude she allowed him in extending her power in Ireland. It was Sussex who briefed her on the Butler-Geraldine split; of the two the Butlers were the more loyal, but the Earl must not be allowed to dominate. Sussex advised the queen on how to discipline Shane O'Neill. MacCarthy Mór and O'Donnell should be created earls. As early as 1562 Sussex realised the need to extend local government over the country by establishing presidencies in Munster and Connaught, by appointing sheriffs, coroners and lesser officers in the newly-established shire grounds. He introduced a series of prerogative courts with the setting up of the Courts of Presidents of Munster and Connaught, and the Court of Castle Chamber modelled on the Star Chamber in England and both he and Sir Henry Sidney recognised the importance of extending English law and institutions to outlying parts of Ireland.

Elizabeth maintained an abiding interest in Ulster. When Con O'Neill died in 1559 the most prudent course for her to have followed was to recognise Shane O'Neill. This would have meant in practice acknowledging the authority he exerted over the MacMahons, Magennises, Maguires, O'Hanlons and O'Cahans. It was Sussex who suggested to the queen the policy of cultivating O'Neill's allies in the rear, particularly the MacDonnells of the Glen and Kintyre, and by increasing the prestige of the O'Donnells. 'If Shane be over-thrown, all is settled. If Shane settle, all is overthrown.'

In June 1561 the queen moved against Shane O'Neill by proclamation intimating that her patience was coming to an end. Even as preparations for war were going on, Elizabeth sent an invitation to Shane to come to London for negotiations. O'Neill proved a tough bargainer. He requested generous expenses for his intended visit and permission for the Earl of Kildare to accompany him. He was prepared to admit allegiance on condition that his autonomy be respected. Elizabeth and Sussex desired a different solution: O'Neill's hegemony would be replaced by fragmented allegiance to the Crown on the part of O'Neill's allies. Negotiation in London was, in fact, concealed warfare. Yet Shane's visit to London was a success. His dress, his gallowglasses, the ease with which he adapted to his courtly surroundings caused wonder and comment. His association with the Spanish ambassador and his attendance at Mass at the Spanish Embassy caused the English Privy Council some anxiety but the smoothness of Shane's diplomacy gave Cecil little excuse for accusations until Shane was back in Ulster. The main business of the visit, the signing of a treaty, was accelerated by the unexpected killing of Shane's nearest rival, the Baron of Dungannon. Early in May Shane left London for Dublin, the queen's proclamation that he was a good subject accompanying him.

He returned to a war situation. Turlough Luineach, whose followers had killed the Baron of Dungannon, had proclaimed himself O'Neill in Shane's absence. Sussex feared O'Neill would join with the Scots and O'Neill sensed the distrust of Elizabeth's officials. Within a matter of months O'Neill had regained control of his own territory and raided O'Donnell's country as an indication of his independence. Sussex was powerless yet he persisted in conciliating Shane's enemies: Maguire, O'Kelly, O'Donnell, and Turlough Luineach. Shane's triumphant campaign against Sussex ended in November 1563 with the queen's pardon. For a year peace reigned in Ulster. 'Men here hath set forth wheat where none was sown this hundred years, and also in building and other things which tendeth to all quietness, whereat all men in this country do greatly rejoice,' wrote the Dean of Armagh. It was an unstable peace threatened by the Scots of Antrim. Shane O'Neill, in a sudden attack near Ballycastle, defeated the Scots making prisoners of James and Somhairle Buidhe MacDonnell. Though he protested that he acted in the queen's interests both Sussex and Cecil were full of apprehension. 'I think good to stir no sleeping dogs in Ireland until a staff be provided to chastise them if they will bite. Many things in common-weals are suffered that are not like' wrote Cecil as he watched the negotiations Shane was conducting in Scotland and quietly set about out-manoeuvering Shane by his own brand of diplomacy from London.

In October 1565 Henry Sidney was appointed lord deputy. His first task was to coerce Shane O'Neill who, as Bagenal reported in the following spring, held all the country 'from Sligo to Knockfergus and from thence to Carlingford, and from Carlingford to Tredath (Drogheda)'. Cecil, sure at last that he had withdrawn Scottish allegiance from Shane, intimated to Sidney that he might prepare for war.

Shane was aware of the preparations. He increased his diplomatic overtures to Scotland and sent emissaries to the Cardinal of Lorraine and to King Charles of France, speaking the language of the new militant counter-reformation: 'the English heretics, enemies of God and the Roman Church'. He suggested to France 'the joining of Ireland to the French crown' but his diplomacy was of no avail. So the summer passed in intensive preparations on both sides. In August Sidney issued a proclamation against Shane. By late September Sidney was on the borders of Ulster but wherever he went, he found deserted camp-sites. By mid-October Sidney had marched unopposed to the confines of Tyrconnell where Hugh Dubh yielded up to him the great castle of Donegal. Sidney returned to Dublin leaving an English garrison and a loyal O'Donnell in Derry. In all his marches he had not encountered Shane once.

In the following months Sidney admitted that he had more reasons to be optimistic than to be depressed despite his famous grumble: 'how pleasant it is in this time of year with hunger and sore travail to harbour long and cold nights in cabins made of boughs and covered with grass, I leave to your indifferent judgment.' Shane O'Neill was, in reality, hemmed in by O'Donnell and his allies had melted away. For Sidney, the arrival in May 1567 of Alexander Óg MacDonnell, steward of Kintyre was a hopeful augury. Meanwhile O'Donnell drew Shane onwards by plundering Strabane Castle and in a surprise attack on Shane O'Neill at the crossing of Lough Swilly, O'Neill's army was routed. It was decisive. O'Neill's hegemony was smashed. Sidney was able to take 3,000 cattle from close to Dungannon while O'Neill's supporters within Tyrone hurriedly submitted.

Shane, without help, was persuaded by his confidant, Nial Mac Connor to solicit aid from Alexander Óg MacDonnell. Taking his prize prisoner, Somhairle Buidhe MacDonnell with him and accompanied by a few retainers, Shane arrived at the camp of Alexander Óg. He was received with marks of friendship but subsequently hacked to pieces in the course of a banquet. His head was eventually sent to Dublin where Campion recorded that it was still thrust on a stake in Dublin Castle four years later.

The fall of Shane O'Neill revealed the power of the

Tudor state. Even if his final defeat was an unfortunate stroke of fortune, O'Neill's real defeat was political. The superior resources of the Tudor policy of expansion prevailed. Yet to write Shane O'Neill off as an archetypal example of Celtic savage is to do him an injustice. His grasp of diplomacy, his military skill, his authority which he exercised in Ulster, above all his realisation of the nature of the conflict he was involved in with Elizabeth's forces in Ireland, mark Shane O'Neill as an Irish Elizabethan surpassed indeed in moral and intellectual stature by the great Hugh O'Neill but claiming in his own right a certain greatness of achievement.

The beginnings of crisis

The defeat of Shane O'Neill settled nothing as Sidney realised. The whole country was restless and disturbed. It was not only the new mood of the Counter-reformation flooding in like a tide in the 1570s, in Munster there were clear indications of a gathering crisis.

In the Tudor century the Butler family had emerged as the champions of the Crown in Ireland. Thomas, tenth earl of Ormond, (1532–1614), son of James and grandson of Piers Roe received his education with Prince Edward at the English court, and later identified himself with the Cecil, Sussex, Leicester clique. His popularity with Elizabeth his cousin was of an enduring nature and he, in return, placed all his resources and talents at her service. In 1559 the young queen appointed him to the office of Lord Treasurer and later he was created general of the royal forces in Munster.

Ormond's most formidable rival in Munster was Gerald, fourteenth earl of Desmond who succeeded to the vast Desmond territories in 1558. Bitter disputes broke out between the two families despite close ties of kinship and marriage. Sidney was at first sympathetic to Desmond and was rebuked by Elizabeth who instructed him in 1566 to favour Ormond. The following year Gerald, earl of Desmond was arrested and sent, a prisoner, to the Tower of London. His cousin James Fitzmaurice administered his estates in his absence.

Ormond's ambitions were far-reaching but tempered by his loyalty to the queen. Like his father, James, he was ambitious to realise vast claims in every province and in these schemes he was generally successful, overcoming his rival Desmond and even offsetting the indiscretions of his own brothers, Edmund, Piers and Edward.

The developing colonisation schemes in Elizabethan Ireland were attracting land-hungry adventurers and courtiers of varying background. Few affairs jolted the Anglo-Irish nobility as the 'Carew incident'. Ormond's brother, Sir Edmund Butler, held the castle of Cloughgrennan in the Idrone barony. He claimed through his father somewhat deviously from the MacMurrough Kavanaghs. Sir Peter Carew, an adventurer of some adroitness, made a claim on the whole of Idrone by virtue of supposed descent from Raymond Le Gros of Carew (the Carew family had held it until the fourteenth century, when it was won back by the MacMurrough Kavanaghs). In December 1568 the claim was allowed by the Council. Carew then began announcing his claim to a moiety of the kingdom of Cork based on a grant of Henry II. The Desmonds and the MacCarthys were seriously alarmed. If the Earl of Ormond could not withstand the pseudo-legalities of Elizabethan claimants, then who could? Sir Edmund Butler joined in the general outcry.

Previously the brief parliament of 1569 had manifested the growing disquiet of the Anglo-Irish. The Act of Attainder for Shane O'Neill's territories was a warning and set a precedent for all future rebels. Presidencies with special military powers were to be set up in Munster and Connaught. The Shiring Act had an unsettling effect on the members of parliament and for a brief period there emerged an articulate opposition to the government.

The presidency of Munster in the 1570s under the energetic Sir John Perrot was a visible proof of the new forces threatening the House of Desmond and the lords of Munster. In the summer of 1569 James Fitzmaurice broke into open revolt. Sidney thought it was the imprisonment of the Earl of Desmond and his brother that provoked the Munster rebellion but insecurity of land tenure was a dominating factor at this early period. The Butlers immediately joined in but the Earl Thomas detached himself and was appointed General for Munster, to 'banish and vanquish those cankered Desmonds'. Two years later Elizabeth was writing that she 'found it strange' that he had not yet accomplished any notable reduction. 'There are now a thousand more traitors than at his coming.'

The most spectacular incident of the rebellion was the attack made by James Fitzmaurice on Kilmallock, a former Geraldine centre, later held by the English. Its destruction, for it was a rich town, is vividly described in the *Annals of the Four Masters*. Perrot immediately placed a large garrison in the burnt-out-town. It was at Kilmallock that the captured Fitzmaurice finally submitted to Perrot and was forced to prostrate himself on the ground with expressions of public sorrow. Shortly afterwards the queen, anxious for peace, restored the Earl of Desmond and Sir John to their possessions and estates after their long stay in London.

Perrot's severe discipline, rumours of plantation, Fitzmaurice's chagrin at not receiving reward of lands from the earl were contributory factors in the combination which began to form after the arrival of the earl in Kerry. The publication of the papal bull of excommunication against Elizabeth *Regnans in caelis* gave a definite impetus to the militant activity of the counter-reformation. Significantly James Fitzmaurice called the conspiracy 'The Catholic League'. His departure in ·1575 for Europe to solicit help met with encouragement from Pope Gregory

XIII who offered him the English adventurer, Stukely, and a small papal force. With this token, Fitzmaurice tried to muster an army for the invasion of Ireland and eventually landed in Dingle in 1579 with an expedition composed of Italians and Spaniards, some three hundred strong, financed jointly by Pope Gregory XIII and Philip II of Spain. Forthwith Fitzmaurice proclaimed a religious crusade and the presence of the distinguished English scholar, Dr Nicholas Sanders, as papal commissary emphasised the religious aspect of the war. Less than a month later Fitzmaurice was killed in a skirmish with the Burkes of Castleconnell near the Shannon.

Fitzmaurice's death forced the earl of Desmond from a position of aloofness. Desmond had been severely tried in his patience since the coming of Sir William Drury to Munster as president, in 1578. English law had been enforced by means of sheriffs and justices. Drury was determined to force the earl to submit to English authority, ably supported by Pelham then Lord Justice of Ireland performing the duties of lord deputy. Coercion, military regime, and martial law became the pattern in Munster. This was going to be a test case for English officials. 'I give the rebels no breath to relieve themselves, but by one of your garrisons or other they be continually hunted. I keep them from their harvest, and have taken great preys of cattle from them, by which it seemeth the poor people . . . are so distressed, as they . . . offer themselves with their wives and children rather to be slain by the army than to suffer the famine that now in extremity beginneth to pinch them,' Pelham reported to the queen less than a year later.

The Earl of Desmond entered the war reluctantly; he had little military skill. He was immediately proclaimed outlaw and the proclamation was signed by Pelham and among others by seven of the Butlers who hoped to benefit from the forfeiture of Desmond's vast estates. Elizabeth was displeased at the high-handed action of Pelham in proclaiming the earl, but Pelham assured her that Desmond 'in all his skirmishes and outrages since the proclamation cried "Papa", which is the Pope, above even you and your imperial crown.'

It could be argued that the Munster War was forced on the government by the need for guarding Ireland against invasion but the appeal of the Munster rebellion as a crusade was a genuine one. Pope Gregory XIII granted temporal jurisdiction over the city of Limerick and its surrounds to the Earl of Desmond in a brief dated 13 May 1580. Two weeks later he granted 'a plenary indulgence as conceded to Crusaders to all who take up arms against Elizabeth'. Though the earl of Desmond was relying on substantial reinforcements from both Spain and the pope, he appealed to his countrymen 'to join in the defence of our Catholic faith against Englishmen which have overrun our country'.

His appeal was answered. In Leinster, Lord Baltinglass and Fiach Mac Hugh O'Byrne rose in rebellion, and the victory of Glenmalure seemed for a while to augur hopefully for the future. In September 1580 a small force, sent by the pope under Colonel San Joseph landed at Smerwick harbour and occupied an old fort, Dunanoir. Help had come but though the presence of Fray Mateo de Oviedo on board gave the impression that the might of Spain was behind the venture, there was no co-operation between Philip II and Gregory XIII. The fort was immediately besieged. Ormond arrived with a distinguished group of English captains: Raleigh, Zouch and Mackworth. In November San Joseph surrendered to Lord Deputy Grey. The massacre of over five hundred of his soldiers followed. The full story still remains untold, but recent research indicates that San Joseph surrendered at discretion.

News of the disaster spread rapidly. In Leinster Fiach Mac Hugh held out until he received favourable terms. Lord Baltinglass fled to Spain. One by one the Desmond castles had surrendered. Youghal was held by the English. Carrigofoill Castle, Askeaton Castle, Ballylogh Castle were yielded up. James, the younger and more capable brother of the earl, had been captured in a raid, and had been handed over to St Leger. In Cork he was hanged and quartered, and for months, his head placed on a spike near one of the city gates was a grim reminder to all traitors. Sir John of Desmond was ambushed and killed by a spear thrust at the hands of a former servant, Fleming, who had deserted to Zouch, newly come to command the English forces in Munster. Gradually the lords of Munster submitted.

Only Gerald, earl of Desmond now remained; an outlaw by force of circumstances. Yet in letters to Pope Gregory he continually protested his loyalty to the cause of religion, 'fighting that Lutheran the Anglican Queen' as he began a letter dated 1 September 1582. A still later letter in June 1583 requested a papal brief from Gregory nominating Gerald overlord of Desmond. In November of that year he was assassinated. The sordid events of the cattle raid surrounding his death give a ghastly dignity to the unstable and moody earl who was neither a hero like his cousin Fitzmaurice, nor a politician like his nephew the earl of Ormond.

Almost all Munster was laid waste in a war which had brought some of the most distinguished Elizabethan soldiers to Ireland. It was an interminable guerilla warfare with no honours of battle going to either side. As a monarch, Elizabeth was aware of the threat to her rule of what she called 'the unordinate tyranny of Irish captaens'. In Ireland with the Munster War the religious elements in the complex set of factors which marked resistance to Tudor conquest came visibly into play. The drawing together of Gaelic and Anglo-Irish against Elizabeth's administration on a common front of religion narrowed the margins of choice for Irish Catholics in politics and in religion: in politics because as in England Elizabeth required a certain concept of order, organic in structure and founded on the monarchy. In religious matters the Munster War strengthened the conviction of Elizabeth's advisers that Catholicism was synonymous with entering into alliances with the enemies of England. The links that bound Dunanoir to Kinsale were present as certainly as the person of Fray Mateo de Oviedo, participant in both expeditions.

The political implications of the Munster War were far-reaching. Hitherto the death-in-rebellion of a chieftain was held to involve the forfeiture of all his lands to the crown. Most of the professional classes, bards, historians and gallowglasses were dispossessed. The 'literati' in particular suffered for supporting a rebellious chieftain and it is from this period that Gaelic poetry like that of Tadgh Dall O'Higgins, becomes political in a broader sense, widening out from the petty warfare of one Gaelic lord with another to the struggle against the superior and more cunning forces of 'the foreigner'. With the death of the Earl of Desmond confiscation of property was now seen to involve the territory of an Anglo-Irish family. The four hundred year old inheritance of the Geraldines was declared forfeit to the queen. Henceforth the main lines of procedure for plantation were laid down, first by Elizabeth, then by James I.

The extent of the Desmond territory, their claims and titles was an intricate one because in addition to the royal grant of Norman times, the 'House of Desmond' had accumulated vast tracts in central Kerry, through north Cork, across Limerick and into Waterford and Tipperary. They put forward well-founded claims to supremacy over native Irish lordships, in particular, MacCarthy Mór and MacCarthy Reagh who, in turn, exercised sway over west Cork and south Kerry.

The question now arose concerning the actual extent of

land that would accrue to the Crown by the attainder of the Earl of Desmond and his allies. Dr Bonn, the German historian on Irish colonisation problems, estimated that 577,000 acres fell to the Crown by the two Acts passed (*Elizabeth* Chaps, 7 & 8) attainting the Earl and his adherents by name but immediately disputes sprang up concerning the legal status of freeholders and those who could produce ancient charters proving title to their lands before Desmond claimed them.[4] The Cogans, Cantons, Poers, Carews and Capels or Supels protested. In the case of Irish lords attainted by name, MacCarthy Mór had supported the Crown forces and had driven some of his sub-chieftains over to Desmond as a result. A number of minor Mac-Carthys were accordingly attainted, as well as O'Donoghue of Ross and O'Mahony of Kinelmeaky. This type of attainder proved to be a legal problem of some consequence. Hitherto none of these Gaelic sub-rulers held any titles from the Crown valid in English law, yet in this case it was argued that they held the whole territory over which they ruled in demesne and therefore by the attainder of the rulers, the lands of all their followers fell to the Crown. At this stage MacCarthy Mór intervened and protested that since he claimed overlordship, the lands should pass back to him. He won his case thanks to the skill of his lawyers and a Kerry jury but his need of money forced him to mortgage the lands to the new claimants, the Brownes, leaving them in temporary possession of the disputed territory. On the death of MacCarthy Mór, the Brownes secured a Crown grant securing the lands to them. In the following chapter the plantation of Munster will be treated in its social and economic aspects. Here we are concerned with legal machinery employed in confiscation a quarter of a century after the plantation of Leix and Offaly. The growing interest of the Crown lawyers in the legal holding of land indicated the watchfulness of the English monarchy about the ultimate ownership of the land of Ireland. It was still far from being resolved, however, as Queen Elizabeth faced her most powerful and formidable Irish rebel, the earl of Tyrone, the great Hugh O'Neill.

The last great rebellion

There are several ways of looking at the Nine Years War. From the point of view of Elizabeth's government it was a rebellion against the sovereign of England. Its European background of Spanish intervention had far-reaching consequences and became a vital factor in turning O'Neill's lengthy struggle for mastery in Ulster into a major attempt to eliminate English rule from Ireland. It was a unique conflict where the methods of warfare and the opposing forces of English and Irish were well balanced.

After the suppression of the Desmond War, Deputy Perrot proceeded to Ulster to establish the queen's supremacy there. The ordering of Ulster was at that time divided between Sir Henry Bagenal and the Baron of Dungannon, Hugh O'Neill. The first Baron of Dungannon was slain in the succession dispute that followed the death of Con O'Neill. The second baron was killed by Turlough Luineach's followers in 1562, leaving his younger brother, Hugh, as the claimant to Con O'Neill's lands in opposition to Shane. Hugh O'Neill was brought by Deputy Sidney to England to be educated. To all appearances he became English and he served under the queen's banner in the Irish wars when he returned. He joined the earl of Essex in his futile effort to colonise Antrim and Down in 1573 and when Sir Henry Sidney was appointed deputy in 1575, Hugh O'Neill hurried to the support of his patron.

Turlough's illness in 1579 opened up the possibility of succession to the position of *The O'Neill* to Hugh O'Neill who imperceptibly began strengthening his position and for over a decade he pursued a devious policy of playing both sides. He petitioned for the lands and title of his grandfather, Con O'Neill and three years later Elizabeth conferred by patent the earldom of Tyrone on him. By the end of the decade all lesser lords in Ulster acknowledged his supremacy, but he desired the name as well. For that he had to wait until death removed Turlough from the office.

Meanwhile Deputy Fitzwilliam had succeeded Perrot after the Munster Plantation. In his opinion the English government appeared to enjoy uncontested supremacy in Ireland. The natives he thought had temporarily laid aside any ideas of rebellion or hope of foreign aid. The desire to exploit the land of Ireland was evident in all parts of the country. Elizabethan adventurers regarded Ireland as a country where estates could be appropriated cheaply and a fortune was to be made. Distress was everywhere, and particularly among the northern lords resentment was hardening into resolve. In May 1593 a confederation had been brought together by Hugh O'Donnell, with the help of the titular Primate, Archbishop Magauran. Archbishop James O'Hely of Tuam went to Spain as envoy. That year Maguire of Fermanagh took the field; O'Donnell a year later. Still Hugh O'Neill stood apart despite the warm friendship that had sprung up between himself and Hugh O'Donnell when the latter made his spectacular escape from Dublin Castle and received hospitality at Dungannon on his way back to Tyrone.

Overtures were gradually made to southern lords: to Cahil O'Connor, son of Brian O'Connor Fahy, to Maurice and Thomas Fitzgerald of the House of Desmond and to Edmund Eustace, claimant of the Baltinglass title and an exile. Still no promise of help came from Philip II.

By 1595 the Northern Confederates held Enniskillen, Sligo, Monaghan and the Moyry Pass. At Clontibret Bagenal was defeated but the earl of Tyrone was not yet ready. He submitted to the government and denied that he had dealings with foreign princes though in fact he had been in communication with Philip. A hint of the official uneasiness is supplied by a contemporary report in the state papers: 'If his (O'Neill's) purpose is to rebel it must proceed either with a combination from Spain . . . his rebellion will be the more dangerous and cost the queen more crowns than any other that have forgone him since Her Majesty's reign.'

Hugh O'Neill had an agent at the Spanish court and in 1596 Philip II sent an envoy offering help in the war of defence which he, Hugh O'Neill was conducting for the defence of the Catholic religion. Sometime in the latter half of 1595 O'Neill undertook the leadership of the Confederacy. The answer to Spain was to the effect that the two earls, Tyrone and Tyrconnell, had been on the point of concluding a treaty of peace with the queen. They would as a result of Philip's communication, renew the war.

Several other emissaries came to confer with the earls during that year. The big question was where would the Spanish troops land but King Philip wished also to be satisfied that there was co-operation and harmony among the Confederates. Limerick was chosen as a suitable landing site or possibly Galway. On the continent the Hapsburg war with France was going against Philip and Elizabeth's fleet was vigilant along the channel. Many fruitless expeditions set out from Spain and never reached Ireland; in 1597 one of these was Padilla's which was driven back by storms in October of that year.

The following year Philip II was dead, leaving a bankrupt Spain as a legacy to his inexperienced son. The treaty of Vervins brought peace between France and Spain. It was however in the Netherlands that the real struggle to throw off the yoke of Spain took place. Philip III was ready to make peace but Queen Elizabeth had English troops helping the Dutch and peace remained elusive. Suddenly Philip changed his plans. The arrival of the Franciscan, Fray Mateo de Oviedo, nominated archbishop of Dublin, as an envoy from the earl of Tyrone decided Philip to divert a fleet he had collected for the Netherlands to

Ireland. Elizabeth was over seventy and this expedition might force her to make peace and withdraw her troops from the Netherlands.

Kinsale was the disastrous result. For Spain it meant the peace of London; for Hugh O'Neill it spelt submission to a queen the fact of whose death was concealed from him until the treaty was made. For Ireland it signified total reconquest under a Stuart king, especially when the Flight of the Earls in 1607 gave unlimited opportunity for the plantation of Ulster.

For the Confederates from the beginning it was a war of defence. Hugh O'Neill hoped by means of war to force Elizabeth to abandon her policy of reconquest which was spreading through Munster and Connacht. The queen's natural caution, her readiness to compromise – particularly with Hugh O'Neill – the long delays of administration had a delaying effect in this long war.

Yet it was warfare of a skilled and technically high standard. Shane O'Neill had already built up an army but whereas Shane armed his followers, Hugh O'Neill trained his army to handle new kinds of arms, and built up over the years an efficient fighting force modelled on the English army. A number of his men had actually seen service in the government army in Ireland. He was not afraid to use mercenaries and he organised companies of native mercenaries.

O'Neill's main position throughout was defensive and his whole resources were concentrated in avoiding a pitched battle. Skirmishes, sudden ambushes and raids cutting off outlying garrisons were important components of his strategy. Geographical conditions suited his tactics, but his greatest battle, The Yellow Ford, made him realise that for ultimate victory he needed foreign help. His line of defence continued to be that of Ulster south from Lough Neagh to the river Erne and he was still holding that line when the Kinsale defeat changed the whole position.

Though the Munster lords supported O'Neill, in 1600 Munster was a region already subdued and for the English army, warfare there was along familiar lines: along the river valleys capturing castle after castle.

It was to be expected that Elizabeth's generals would force an offensive. According to Dr Hayes-McCoy three phases may be distinguished: that from 1593–97; from 1597–1600; and the final phase, 1600–03.[5] During the first phase the customary method of government warfare was employed: an expedition led by the lord deputy into enemy country, the destruction of land, and the posting of a garrison. It was routine reconnaissance. The strategy of the second phase was an elaboration of the first phase. A three-pronged attack was directed on Ulster from different points. Lord Deputy Mountjoy was responsible for the strategy of the final phase. He too favoured the method of simultaneous attack and established a line of garrisons along the Ulster border at Mount Norris, Armagh, on the Blackwater, at Breifne, Boyle Abbey and Lecale. Then he systematically destroyed the enemy's corn and cut off food supplies. He never relaxed his pressure, campaigning through the winter. He even landed troops by sea in Derry in the north. An Irish victory at Kinsale would not have ended the war; it would have prolonged it.

Mountjoy's career as deputy 1601–03 was successful. He dominated the political and administrative complexities of the Irish scene to a remarkable degree during his brief period of deputyship and gave the reconquest of Ireland a definite direction. He made no secret of the fact that he wanted peace in Ireland which would be a peace of reconciliation and assimilation. A dedicated soldier he was a careful strategist and it is generally agreed that his part in the Kinsale campaign made it the decisive phase in Irish history that it was. Possibly the ruthlessness with which he is associated in our history was not cruelty but the strict consequence of his military commitments. His brief deputyship marks a watershed between the indeterminate nature of the English conquest begun under Henry VIII and the domination by the Stuart kings and their officials over the whole island in the seventeenth century.

5 Plantation and the Irish countryside

The Origins of Colonisation

The kind of change which Tudor colonisation brought to the Irish countryside provides the clues to understanding how a society mainly pastoral and tribal, passed into a structure recognisably modern. Efforts to transform the Irish countryside by establishing a network of shires on the English administrative model, by changing the land-holding and law systems, and by the planning of new towns were main factors in the making of the Irish landscape.

Previously the suppression of the religious houses, (some four to five hundred) set in motion by Henry VIII and ratified by the 1536 Irish parliament had begun the process of alteration.[1] It was a gradual but surprisingly speedy transfer of property accompanied by a developing mechanism of legal inquiry which was later used efficiently in the plantation schemes. By 1540 most of the religious houses in the Pale, in the lands of Ormond, and in the southern towns and cities were suppressed.[2] On St Leger's appointment as deputy in 1540, a royal commission was issued to him charging him with the takings of surveys of monastic property now, by the dissolution of the monas-teries, decreed to be royal property.[3]

The Surveys taken at the Dissolution give some indica-tion of the extent of the properties and supply an occasional hint of management, as in the case of Trim friary, in 1542:

Grant to Lewis Tudyr and others, to the use of Anthony Sentleger, Knt., Lord Deputy, in consideration of the sum of £56 of the site of the monastery of friars minors observants of Tyrm, a garden without a portchgate, the Mawdlen chapel, the Mawdlen church-yard, an ell weir on the Boyne, a park extending from the weir to lynces park, land extending from the river to Saint Thomas' park . . .[4]

In England the dissolution had effected a considerable alteration by the fifth decade of the century, not only in the character of the monastic granges but in the mobility of the landholders. In Ireland the *Fiants* of successive Tudor monarchs bear testimony to the absorption of the monastic lands first into the hands of layowners like the Butlers and the Fitzgeralds, and then later into the avaricious schemes of the new colonisers. Sir James Hamilton is representative of the process. He received from his cousin James I the vast possessions attached to the Abbey of Bangor, with the title, Viscount Clandeboy. These lands had nominally lapsed to the crown in the reign of Henry VIII but were retained by neighbouring Gaelic lords until the conquest of Ulster made plantation possible. With the reign of James I came the consistent attempt to vest all lands in the Crown, a task eventually accomplished by the Act of Settlement in 1662.

Centuries earlier the Norman colonists had settled along the plains, along the coasts and beside rivers. They left the highlands, the deep woods, the marshy ground and the rich grasslands behind the inaccessible woods to the Gaelic rulers and their peoples. In the early sixteenth century the Irish countryside presented stretches of densely packed oakwoods with undergrowth of holly intermingled with ash, birch, alder and hazel, the whole forming a blanket of natural woodland over the countryside.[5]

The density of the forests may be gauged from local traditions existing west of Galway, in south-west Munster

Map of woodland distribution about 1600

and in the regions around Lough Erne. 'One could walk on the top of the trees from Letterfrack on the west coast to Galway . . . a squirrel could have hopped from Killarney to Cork by leaping from bough to bough . . . a wild cat could have walked on the tops of the trees from Lough Cutra to Creigeen . . .'[6]

Contemporary records bear testimony to the impenetrable thickness of the woodlands. It took Donal O'Sullivan Beare and his men a whole night to pass through a pocket of wood in west Roscommon near the River Suck. Sir John Davies in 1607 described the vast forest which lay to the north-west of Lough Neagh as 'well nigh as large as the New Forest in Hampshire and stored with the best timber in Ireland'. Sir Peter Carew met his death in the great forest which stretched between Charleville and Kilmallock occupying the valley of the Maigue, a wood according to the account 'lined with Irish musketry'. On either side of the Shannon were 'woods and good store of sapling timber'.[7]

By the beginning of the following century the woodlands were shaded into the maps of the conquerors and were marked for destruction. They had proved a grave obstacle to colonisation and the possibility of their exploitation for the timber industry became an added inducement to settlers.

In a series of articles on colonisation D. B. Quinn has drawn attention to 'the alternating influences of tough and not-so-tough English policy which moulded painfully the face and structure of Ireland'.[8] Henry VIII and his deputies, on the whole, pursued a conciliatory policy in the attempt to reconquer Ireland. By the middle of the sixteenth century plantation as an arm of conquest made its appearance in official policy. Sir James Crofts, Lord Deputy 1551–2, recommended a plantation based around a central garrison core as local buffer in the borders of the Pale along the Shannon. His ideas were expanded by Lord Deputy Sussex and the Act(s) known as the Third and

Fourth Philip and Mary was passed in the Irish parliament of 1557, establishing the legal basis for the plantation of Leix-Offaly.

The brief extracts from official correspondence in the *Calendar State Papers Ireland* for the years 1550–80 conceal the ongoing discussion about ways of establishing English settlement in Ireland. Among the earlier group of Elizabethans actively interested in Irish colonial schemes were William Cecil, the earls of Leicester and Sussex, Sir Thomas Smith, Sir Henry Sidney and Sir William Fitzwilliam; later in the 1570s the issues were widened by Sir Richard Grenville, Warham St Leger, Sir Walter Raleigh and Walter Deveraux, first earl of Essex. What marks the discussion is the progression from military preoccupations to social and economic aspects of colonial policy in the years 1564–75.[9]

To be a real colony it was argued increasingly by the second group, settlement must be of a permanent nature, fairly intensive, consisting of different types of settlers. There should be provision for new towns and villages and schemes for pushing local administration further into the country while trading outlets would simultaneously be explored. In the late sixties there began in Ulster and Munster a number of private projects by syndicates of private gentlemen, that of Sir Thomas Smith in the Ards being the most widely known.[10] Though unsuccessful a growing body of information about the Irish countryside was being made available.

The shiring process

Side by side with the colonial absorption of Ireland went the shiring process of the whole country. A memorial of 1537 begins:

> Because the country called Leinster and the situation thereof is unknown to the King and his council, it is to be understood that Leinster is the fifth part of Ireland.

According to Sir John Davies, the shiring of Ireland was first attempted in the reign of King John when twelve shires were designated in Leinster and Munster. From that time to the mid-sixteenth century, no permanent counties were delimited, indeed the vagueness of the territorial boundaries of the existing shires indicated the diminishment of effective English control during the late middle ages. Stanihurst complained that the boundaries of the English Pale were 'cramperned and crouched into an odd corner of the country named Fingal, with a parcel of the king's land of Meath and the counties of Kildare and Louth'.[11]

With the plantation of Leix-Offaly the process of shiring was again pursued energetically. During the reign of Elizabeth I the counties Longford, Clare, Galway, Sligo, Mayo, Roscommon, Leitrim, Armagh, Monaghan, Tyrone, Coleraine, Londonderry, Donegal, Fermanagh and Cavan were formed. Their division was tentative, Sir Arthur Chichester, Lord Deputy to James I, completing the shiring of Ireland. According to Sir John Davies, the process was accomplished by 1616 though he comments:

> the whole realm being divided into shires, every bordering territory doubt was made in what country the same should lie was added or reduced to a country certain.[12]

More sophisticated in method than the earlier medieval efforts, Tudor shiring was accompanied by the intensive use of inquisition, delimitation of area by surveying, and by mapping. Thomas Blennerhasset combines eloquence with practicality in his observations about the Maguire territory during the inquisition prior to shiring:

> The county of Fermanagh, sometimes Maguire's country, rejoice. Many undertakers, all incorporated in mind as one, they with their followers, seek and are desirous to settle themselves. Woe to the wolf and the

wood kerne! The islands of Lough Erne shall have habitations, a fortified corporation, market towns and many new erected manors shall now so beautify her desolation that her inaccessible woods, with spaces made tractable, shall no longer nourish devourers, but by the sweet society of a loving neighbourhood shall entertain humanity even in the best society.[13]

Land measurements

The intensive legislation which accompanied the plantation schemes exposed the anomalies of land tenure in sixteenth-century Ireland. The survival of an older system of land-holding side by side with the Anglo-Norman system of land tenure had, by the sixteenth century, rendered the units of land-division indistinct and complex. In Irish law, land was owned by a class of free landowning families. These Gaelic rulers were a nobility whose followers occupied their holdings with a status little higher than that of tenant-at-will in English law, and far less precise. In the English lordships the feudal system as modified by English customs, and later still by Irish usage, operated.

By the end of the fifteenth century the fiscal unit was the carucate or 'ploughland' of 120 acres of arable land, excluding all 'rivers, meadows, mores, pastures and hylls and wodds', and giving allowance for pasturage at the rate of grazing per 300 cows on every 'towne' of eight ploughlands. Begley in his *Diocese of Limerick* calculated that the Desmond Survey adopted the carucate to consist of eighty acres of arable land according to Irish measure. Considerable flexibility then occurred in land measurements. For instance in Gaelic parts of Munster 'ploughlands' were still the measure estimated by an area's capacity to carry cattle, or by the extent of its arable land measured by the number of days it took to plough as late as the second Munster plantation.[14]

Infield and outfield in Gaelic Ireland

A region of the Pale from the air

Efforts to transform the older Gaelic land measurements into English acreage continued to baffle surveyors; even Petty, despite elaborate precautions, fell victim to miscalculation. Elizabethan surveyors came to rely on the *townland* or *baile* as a land unit useful for plotting plantation grants, in a manner similar to the use of the *triucha cet* for the admeasurement of a barony in the shiring process.[15] The townland was a land-unit large enough to support a number of small farmers and its size was usually delimited by local landmarks such as mountains, streams, bogs or by the crossing of an ancient track. In Munster the townland was referred to as 'ploughlands', in Ulster as 'balliboes', and in Fermanagh and Monaghan as 'tates'.

The chief method of eliciting information under oath from the older inhabitants was the Court of Inquisition. The Normans had introduced the inquisition record as a form of inventory. Henry VIII had re-introduced it at the dissolution of the monasteries and it was adopted by successive Tudor administrators as part of the machinery for plantation schemes. The inquisition records were essential factors for the mapping of sixteenth-century Ireland. It was the maps, however, which unlocked the secrets of the Irish countryside.

Mapping the countryside

The desire for visualised measurement and for quantification which marked the age of discovery gave a new impetus to the art of map-making. The publication, in 1564, of the Mercator Map of England and Wales offered to English surveyors and draughtsmen the incentive to produce maps of progressively better quality. The Elizabethan collection of maps are noteworthy for their draughtsmanship and artistry. Maps of Ireland have their place in these collections, sometimes annotated in the hand of Cecil. The Irish maps of John Goghe, Francis Jobson, Bartlett, Robert Lythe, John Browne, Boazio and Norden display the gradual improvement in technique. Devices such as triangulation, the adoption of the plane table, the use of the compass rose, and later the popularity of the circumferuntur, particularly by Bartlett makes this period a splendid age of cartography in Ireland.[16]

The mapping of Ireland assumed greater significance as frequent rebellion during Elizabeth's reign brought complete conquest of the island in sight. The clear presentation of topographical details are features of the military surveys which accompanied the Nine Years' War, step by step, into Ulster. Sir John Perrot's rueful comments described the Moyry Pass as 'a broken causey besette on both sydes with bogges, where the Irish might skyppe but the English could not goe; and at the two endes it was naturally fenced with short and shrubbed wood'. This was skilfully translated by the penmanship of Francis Jobson into a track running through wooded country, trees and shrubs being principally identified as beech, hazel, willow and thorn.[17]

A comparison between the crude map of John Goghe and Boazio's Map of Ireland (1603) followed by an examination of Bartlett's war charts for Mountjoy has the effect of seeing a jig-saw being pieced together. As Professor Hayes-McCoy remarks: 'If we look upon Bartlett's earlier maps as records of the progress of the English towards victory and their lacunas as evidence of the stubborness of the resistance encountered, Bartlett's later ones are symbols of Irish defeat. They are cartographical proof of the ultimate overthrow of O'Neill.'[18]

Roads and Communications

The biggest problem for mapmakers in Tudor Ireland was that of surveying in a country at war where roads were bad or non-existent. It was a moment of supreme achievement when Mountjoy, according to Fynes' *Itinerary*, succeeded in cutting a path through 'a small pace or skirt of wood' to reach Doundavalla on the south bank of the Erne. There

Bartlett's map of the Moyry Pass

six miles away was O'Neill's fortress at Dungannon
hitherto impregnable behind its shelter of woods and bogs.

The historical development of roads in medieval Ireland
served regions and to a large extent roads were controlled
by regional topography. Ordinarily no English force in
sixteenth-century Ireland attempted to move otherwise
than by a recognised road, or by one prepared in advance.
The mountain pass, the forest pathway, the *togher* or cause-
way running through a bog feature constantly in Irish
military history at this period. The bridge at Leighlin in
County Carlow was the main passage across the River
Barrow, linking the government in Dublin with the
counties of Kilkenny, Waterford, Cork, Limerick and
Kerry. Wexford was also dependent on Leighlin Bridge
for entrance into the Pale, so menacing were the attacks of
the O'Tooles and the O'Byrnes in the Wicklow mountains.

Though travel by water was much faster, and in peace-
time was favoured by travellers, the military character of
the Tudor conquest made travelling by land a necessity.

There appears a growing preoccupation in the state papers with the building of bridges and roads. Sidney's 'Description of the Provinces of Ireland' (C. 1580 cf. *Sloane MS* 2,200, Brit. Mus.) is full of references to schemes for constructing bridges.

'I gave order for the making of a bridge of Athlone which I finished, a piece found serviceable; I am sure durable it is, and I think memorable.' The bridge over the Suck at Ballinasloe 'being the common passage to Galway' was constructed by Sir Nicholas Malby under Sidney's direction.

Many clues about the impassable nature of the Irish countryside may be picked up from the dispatches and maps of the Nine Years' War. In Bartlett's war charts of Ulster the new military roads for the English troops run through cornfields enhancing the impression that the routes of sixteenth-century roads depended upon the kind of rock or soil over which they ran. Nor do we find any examples of great engineering skill employed at this period. The military road to Castleisland across Slieve Loughra was laboriously begun after the Desmond rebellion. It ran directly from one military point of observation to another with little reference to the nature of the country. Though the Elizabethan plan included Liscarroll along the route, more than forty years later we read in a contemporary account of the siege of Liscarroll Castle in 1642 of the soldiers 'dragging along with them their battering piece in a piece of timber hewn hollow, with twenty-five yoke of oxen, over bogs where wheels would have sunk, and where no carriage had ever been known to pass'.[19]

It was not until the Parliament of 1614 that the Highways Act set in motion the system of roads which were constructed right through that century. 'This day, (1 May 1615) Mr. Baron Elyot and Mr. Sollicitor brought a Bill from

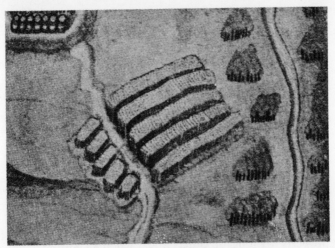

A military road driven through a field of ripe
corn sown in wide ridges

the lords for amending of Bridges and Toghers.'[20] It was a modest beginning but a revolutionary one, for the new roads of Munster and Ulster were to be constructed as a network of communications between the plantation towns. As such they played a major part in the development of the new boroughs. All that was in the future. The construction of roads continued to be impeded by the constant rebellions and by resistance to the planters. Paradoxically it was the continuing need for military routes and the resourcefulness of the new planters which made the roads of seventeenth-century Ireland a reality.

The Munster Plantation

At the beginning of the seventeenth century the most advanced parts of Ireland from the planters' point of view were Leinster and Munster. Colonisation had taken place in about half of Queen's County, one third King's County. Considerable plantations were taking root in Munster, in the conquered lands of the earl of Desmond. Plantation was also being essayed haphazardly in parts of Connaught, Tipperary and Clare.

Some centuries earlier the Desmond Palatinate had become an organised state where feudal and Gaelic customs merged into each other in an elaborate pattern of relationships with the earl of Desmond, sovereign lord of Norman vassal and Gaelic sub-chieftain alike. Originally the Desmond possessions were divided into manors, in each of which the chief lord had a castle and a certain amount of land known as the demesne. It was an intricate political geography of Munster designed to yield a revenue on lands for the sovereign lord, and then in descending scale, for each of his sub-chieftains. As in the case of Leitrim cited in the state papers: 'not one acre of land but is owned properly by one or other, and each man knows what belongs to himself.'[21]

The attainder of Gerald, 16th earl of Desmond, in the reign of Elizabeth opened up an important chapter in the history of colonisation. The death-in-rebellion of a Gaelic chieftain was held to involve the forfeiture of all the lands of his clan to the Crown. On the death of Earl Gerald who was regarded by the Crown as a chief-in-rebellion, the four hundred year old inheritance of that Norman family – some half million acres, was declared forfeit to the Crown. An elaborate plan was drawn up for peopling Munster with 'loving subjects of good behaviour and account, none of the meer Irish to be maintained in any family'. Orders were given for surveys and maps and the 'Desmond' Surveys are a testimony to the industry of the paper plantation of Munster.

The first Desmond Survey was undertaken by commissioners appointed in 1584 to examine the lands forfeited as a result of the Earl's death in rebellion. It deals principally with the counties of Limerick and Kerry and it supplies valuable information on the older divisions of the land, the baile, the cantred, and the carucate. The Survey deals with ownership, location, nature and extent of the regions surveyed and indicates the services traditionally payable to the earl of Desmond. It furnishes a picture of the palatinate in decline but still in outline faithful to the early vigour of the Desmonds' ability to administer their vast estates.

The second Desmond Survey or Peyton Survey was undertaken in 1598 after the death of Donal MacCarthy, first earl of Clancarty. The Peyton Survey deals mainly with south Kerry and south west Cork and throws much light on the political and social geography of a great native lordship. The locations and extent of the lands of the chief native families are described and a description of the rents and services due to MacCarthy is given. It supplies details of fisheries, mines and forests, and is accompanied by some fine illustrations.[22]

Francis Jobson, one of the main cartographers of the Munster Plantation, has left us the boundaries of the new seignories on his plantation maps and Dr D. B. Quinn points out that it should be possible to discover the basic outline of the first settlement.[23] Dr Quinn has suggested a basic figure of 86 households in each seignory of the twenty envisaged in 1586 and he has tentatively calculated a plantation population of around 8,000 persons. For ten years the new plantation remained a problematic success with groups of settlers occupying seignories in the rich lands of north Munster. Then came the advance of the Nine Years War into Munster bringing wholesale disruption to the settlers. The final period 1602–22, was a period of restoration, incorporating the further plantation of the Mac Carthy lands in south west Munster. An influential group of landlord undertakers settled permanently in Munster: Richard Boyle, George Courtney, Arthur Hyde, Edward Denny.

Munster already possessed fine port-towns whose developed harbours and established trade connections were now used by the planters. In addition a number of

Youghal in the time of Sir Walter Raleigh

new plantation towns came into being or were re-built from former ruins as in the case of Tralee. Killarney, Bandonbridge, Mallow and Tallow were energetically set up with houses of English type by local undertakers around which in time Irish dwellers settled. In contrast to the towns of the Ulster Plantation planning seems to have been haphazard and little attention, except in the case of Bandonbridge, was paid to lay-out.

Housing and Farming in Munster

Plantation experience was dearly bought in Munster. No building connected with the first settlement so far has been identified and Spenser's 'fair stone house' was completely destroyed. The need for effective defence of the new plantation continued for many decades. Lack of roads and the slowness of cannon to adapt to Irish conditions kept in continuance the military importance of the Irish castle whose great block form with rounded angle towers dominated the Munster landscape. The planters had little choice but to study the existing tower-house with its enclosure or 'bawn' so long a residence and fortress for Irish and Anglo-Norman gentlemen in the declining days of the English Lordships. The ground plan of the new mansions of the planters derived from Irish as much as from English sources. Despite the semi-fortified character of the buildings they manage a surprising variety in plan. In general their symmetrical lay-out and the insertion of large multi-light windows and many-gabled roof line were features brought from the Renaissance architecture popular in late sixteenth-century England, as in the Butler House in Carrick-on-Suir. Kanturk House in County Cork and Burntcourt in County Tipperary were oblong with large projecting square angle-towers. Ightermurragh and Kilmaclenine were oblong with smaller lateral wings. Ballea House in County Cork was designed as an L-shaped house. The planters' mansions were ambitiously large: Kanturk (80′ × 33′); Mallow (80′ × 27′); Burntcourt was still incomplete in 1641 and was gutted like Wentworth's Jinglestown.[24]

The Butler House at Carrick-on-Suir

The planters brought with them the English plough and engaged extensively in tillage. They brought English stock, cows, bulls, sheep, mares and stallions as is evident from the request of John Thornburgh, 'to transport with me fiftie Ewes, eight Rammes, six mares, twentie Cowes and tow bulls for myne Owne breede . . .'[25] Plantation farmsteads, of which few hints survive, were modelled on those of the West Country where undertakers recruited yoemen planters extensively. By the second decade of the seventeenth century, the plantation had taken root. Woods were hacked away and the countryside and its people were exploited. Basically it was a landlord plantation which materially affected the landscape and culture of Munster.

The conquest of Ulster

'One thinks of the hare that haunts the wood,/ And of the salmon in the bay;/Even the wild bird; one grieves to thinks they are abroad./Then one remembers Hugh Maguire/Abroad in a strange land.'[26]

The intense feeling with which Eochy O'Hussey portrays the Fermanagh chieftain, Hugh Maguire, making his way to the battle of Kinsale through the ice-swept Munster countryside conveys the anguish of besieged Ulster before its final capitulation. More than any other part of Ireland Ulster had presented the challenge of conquest to English colonisers. In that region the three greatest Gaelic Lordships occupied most of the territory, ruling by the sword, defying English law, holding on to a way of life where the military and the pastoral found expression in the 'hosting', the 'creaghting' and the 'Booleying'. Here indeed was a countryside where cattle were the symbols of war and wealth.[27]

The attention with which Elizabethan statesmen were regarding Ulster is evidenced by the corrections made by Lord Burghley on the contemporary maps of Ireland and by the interest shown in Marshal Bagenal's 'Description

Tullaghoge, territorial centre of the kingship of the O'Neills

of Ulster Anno 1586'. Information was steadily augmented through the following decade: 'Dobbs MS Description of Antrim C.1589', Bartlett's war-maps of Mountjoy's campaign and Sir John Davies' comments on 'Munster and Ulster 1606' being among the best accounts.

The Flight of the Earls of Tyrone and Tyrconnell presented a golden opportunity to the Crown. Scottish and English settlers were invited by King James I to colonise the escheated lands already in the process of being shired. The 'countries' of the Gaelic Lordships now became the counties of Armagh, Cavan, Donegal, Fermanagh, Londonderry, and Tyrone. The City of London Companies acquired proprietorship of Coleraine. Previously Down and Antrim had been the scene of earlier colonising enterprises like that of Sir Thomas Smith of the Ards, and once again they became areas of active colonial experiment around the Lagan valley.[28]

In the escheated counties conditions of plantation varied in proportion to the amount of land allotted to a grantee.

Undertakers of 2,000 acres were to hold their lands by knight's service *in capite* and were required to build a strong castle and strong court or bawn. Servitors with lots of 1,500 acres were to hold them by knight's service as of the Castle of Dublin and were obliged to build a stone or brick house with a bawn. Those who received 1,000 acres each held their lands by common soccage and were required to build a bawn within two years. Power was given to erect manors and land customs such as freeholding were introduced together with English forms of land tenure.[29]

The most striking change which the plantation introduced into the landscape of Ulster was the layout of new towns and villages. Hitherto the Gaelic settlements of huts, built around the ruler's castle as in Dungannon, were impermanent structures, to be removed and rebuilt elsewhere as required. In 1603 there were only two towns of note, Carrickfergus and Newry. In the plantation scheme provision was made for twenty-three new towns, land being set aside for that purpose, throughout the new counties.

Derry

The plan of the towns formed a 'grid' pattern: a central square on which the public buildings like the courthouse, the gaol, the town hall were situated. From the square or 'diamond' the streets ran, straight and wide, to form the grid, with walls surrounding the enclosed space. Three towns in particular became the main centres of the planter region: Londonderry, Belfast and Enniskillen. The 1615 Highways Act initiated the building of roads joining the new towns.

Gradually in the subsequent years of the reign of James I, plantations took place in Longford, Wexford, Leitrim, Ely O'Carroll, but as the Chief Justice, Sir John Davies prophesied gloomily in 1613 rebellion still smouldered, to burst into flames forty years later. Meanwhile, for the planters and their tenants there was land to be tilled and new forms of agriculture to be introduced.

Fields and Farming

Only in the Pale is there systematic evidence that feudal ways of working the land were successfully established.

The Norman settlers had introduced into the Pale the three-field system with ditch-banks separating the farms. The Ordinances for the Government of Ireland in 1534 decreed that 'every husbandman having a plough within the English Pale shall set by the year twelve ashes in the ditches and closes of his farm.' Gradually the ditch-bank, lined with stones between which the ash was rooted, became the popular form of ditch in the lowlands as the planters moved in.

The inherent flexibility of settlement in the Gaelic parts of Ireland makes it difficult to describe field boundaries during the sixteenth century. In a dispatch to the earl of Salisbury (1606) Sir John Davies grumbled that 'a year's ditch passeth for a very strong fence'. The *Advertisements for Ireland* which were aimed at prospective planters state 'the fields lie open and unenclosed. Where wood is plentiful

The hedged ditch

they hedge in all their corn with stakes and bushes and pull them down in the winter and burn them'.[30]

Transhumance embodying the rundale system of working the land was the pastoral kind of agriculture practised in Gaelic parts of Ireland. The *clachan* or clustered house group was the social unit which shared in fragmented ownership. The 'infield' situated near the *clachan* was divided into strips and tilled by the families, carefully fenced with a rail or wattle fence.[31] The main crops were oats with some barley, wheat in the Pale, and rye west of the Shannon in Connacht and Clare. Barley was grown in Wexford and Carlow. The potato came late in the seventeenth century but turnips were sown from the fifteenth century onwards. Clover appeared about the same time.

Beyond the infield stretched the grazing lands of the cattle and sheep known as the 'outfield'. These were the moors, the hilly uplands, the shores of lakes and rivers like Lough Neagh, the Bann, the Shannon and the upper reaches of the Blackwater. The form of transhumance known as 'booleying' which the native Irish practised was a way of life, seasonal yet timeless, idyllic in its customs, cruelly practical in its assertion of ownership rights.[32]

Ploughing by the tail was the primitive form of ploughing and shocked the stranger in Ireland who recoiled from his encounter with the spectacle of five or six men, an equal number of horses tied by the tail to the short Irish plough, all engaged in tilling the rough stony fields. Many efforts were made to have it discouraged. An Act of the Council of Ireland in 1606 forbade the custom and imposed a stiff fine but the House of Commons reported that the custom still existed in 1615.

By the beginning of the seventeenth century the area under pasturage was much greater than that under tillage in Ireland. By then it was a depopulated country in which decades of war had interfered with the normal practice of husbandry. In 1589 Payne had written that 'a fat pigge, one pound of Butter, or ii gallons of new milk, for a penny; a redde deare, without the skinne, for iis vid; a fat Beefe for xiii s iiid; a fat mutton for xvs iiid.' English law came to the Munster countryside when game laws were introduced forbidding the shooting of 'deare, hare, partridge and pheazant', and ordering ditches and hedges 'to be planted with double course of quickset'. The red deer attracted the admiration of all visitors to Ireland. Fynes Moryson spoke of them 'loosely scattered' in the woods of the Earl of Ormond. Camden's *Brittania* described the County of Mayo as 'rich in cattle, deer, hawks and honey'. The natural woodlands were being cut down but the planters were setting new types of trees in their farmyards or closes: the sycamore, the beech, the elm which had become practically extinct in Ireland, and the lime tree. There are references to horse breeding in the letters of James I and to stud farms like that of Sir Bernard Grenville in Munster, but on the whole according to Wentworth animal breeding was still backward in the decade before 1641.

Though there was no large scale drainage scheme like that of the Fens in England, there is evidence of drainage in fields both within the Pale and in the Gaelic parts of Ireland. The hen's foot system was most commonly employed, and small channels were dug down slope. Manuring of the land was primitive as is evident from the comments of Sir John Davies but to offset the deficiencies caused by any quick method of spreading manure, the infield of a *clachan* was often situated on sloping land, and the manure was placed at the highest point, and allowed to move downwards in channels dug for the purpose.

Conclusions

The period 1541–1641 was a formative one in the making of the planters' countryside. It commenced with the sudden availability of the monastic lands. It was not the Crown which immediately profited but powerful families like the Butlers and other Anglo-Irish lords. Little research has been done on the consequences of the Dissolution in Gaelic parts but the negotiations known as Surrender and Regrant would suggest that the Gaelic lords were aware of the kinds of annexation open to them by formally submitting to Henry VIII. As the century of plantation wore on, these acquisitions were in turn absorbed into the schemes of the new colonisers, Boyle, earl of Cork readily coming to mind.

It was the age when inquisition records, patent and close rolls, surveys and mapping projects itemised the Irish countryside on an intensive scale and brought to increasing efficiency the methods employed by Sir William Petty in the Civil Survey which was the prelude to the massive Cromwellian plantation. Running like a thread through the surveys were the old land measurements of the 'plough-land' the 'townland', and the transformed Triucha Cet – the barony.

It was a century which saw the shiring process of Ireland completed and a network of boroughs beginning to spread throughout the island. The creation of the boroughs included tolls and the right to hold fairs and markets, as well as corporate property. The boroughs began to play a significant part in the unsettled and disrupted social geography of seventeenth-century Ireland. The social unit of the lordship became the new region of the county. The growth of towns and their diversification is a marked feature of this period and together with the clearance of the woodlands and the building of roads left the most permanent marks on a countryside scored deeply during the whole of the period under review with the scars of warfare.[33] For when all is written it was a countryside hacked out by the planter. Landscaping when it came in the next century was a leisure occupation of the victorious colonists.

6 The struggle for constitutional rights

The reign of James I

In 1603 by the death of Queen Elizabeth I, James VI of Scotland found himself king of England including Wales, and king of Ireland. For the first time all three kingdoms had a distinct and separate juridical relationship exercised through councils and parliaments with the same monarch. King James was pre-eminently a Scot and he brought with him to London a wealth of practical shrewdness derived from some twenty years of ruling Scotland. In Scotland the 1590s had marked the end of an era for the feudal character of Scottish society. Never again did a faction of the nobles, of themselves, challenge the Crown. In Ireland the failure of the Nine Years War and the flight of the northern earls to Europe diverted attention from the central feature of those early years of King James' rule over Ireland: the gradual pressure on Gaelic society to yield way to the application of English Common Law and to the shiring process of the whole country. Though King James came from an alien system of law and government and had little sympathy with English liberties and customs, his officials in Ireland, Sir John Davies in particular, were in the mainstream of the development of common law which upheld the parliament as source and the common law courts as interpreters of that law. It was the lawyer who established the terms of reference for the constitutional struggle of the seventeenth century in Ireland.

The close connections between Ulster and Scotland were more immediate to James than to any of his Tudor predecessors. He recognised that the relationship which existed between the Scottish barons and their dependants was quite similar to those that existed between the Gaelic lords and their followers. He had already achieved his aim of extending the power of the central government in Edinburgh into the Scottish Border, into the Highlands and across the Western Isles. By 1597 he was effecting a policy of infiltrating lowland Scots among the recalcitrant highlanders. Lewis was declared forfeit to the Scottish Crown and a number of Scottish gentlemen undertook to establish themselves there as colonists among the 'utterly barbarous' islanders. For James I the problem of dealing with the Ulster lands confiscated by his Dublin government and the Scottish problem of the south-west were connected. The close and friendly alliances between the highlanders and the Ulster Irish were undesirable to the new monarch of Britain and Ireland. A significant stage of breaking those connections was reached in 1608 when James had the island chiefs of the Western Isles imprisoned by a trick. It was an event which coincided with the suppression of Sir Cahir O'Doherty's rebellion in Inishowen by Sir Arthur Chichester. The subsequent resolution by James and Chichester to treat the native Irish landholders more severely than originally planned was similar to James' efforts to crush his rebellious subjects in the highlands.

The Ulster plantation was the most ambitious plantation so far. Six escheated counties were mapped out; wherever possible, native Irish were to be transferred from the planted lands, and English and Lowland Scots settlers were invited to settle. The Scots showed a readiness to colonise which was lacking among English tenantry in previous plantations. A high proportion of the new tenant settlers in Donegal, Down and Antrim were Scottish. Though the joint-stock enterprise of the London Companies has commanded attention from historians and was,

in many respects, the most efficient in colonising Londonderry and Coleraine, the plantations of Montgomery and
Hamilton in Down and Antrim approximated most
closely to the aspirations of James I in extending the
influence and characteristics of the thrifty Lowland Scot.
With the plantation of Ulster a distinctive group was
inserted into seventeenth-century Irish society, different
not only in race but in religion from the English settlers
who were their co-colonists. The Scots laid the foundation
of the Presbyterian Church which rapidly assumed the role
of Protestant nonconformity vis-a-vis the Established
Church of Ireland. Scottish ministers took up residence in
parish churches belonging to the Established Church and
made no secret of their Presbyterian convictions. In the
cases of Robert Blair minister of Bangor and John
Livingston who secured a curacy at Killinchy, James
Hamilton, Lord Clandeboy, was influential in their
appointments and was in sympathy with their Presbyterian
aspirations. Gradually the Scots in Ulster built up a colony
of sizeable proportions. By 1640 it was estimated that there
were about 40,000 Scots in Ulster out of a population in
Ireland roughly estimated at less than a million.

The country now entered a time of uneasy peace with
the Dublin administration effective for the first time over
the whole island. The semi-autonomous lordships had
disappeared; every Irish landholder found a settler's
residence within his range. The reign of the first Stuart king
witnessed an intensive securing of land tenures on the part
of the new settlers and a growing insecurity among those
older inhabitants who were still in possession of lands
anciently held by their families or clans.

The Old Irish

Numerically the native Irish formed the bulk of the population but the disarray caused by the defeat of their leaders
at Kinsale and the subsequent emigration of many of the

leaders to Europe left the people without power or initiative. To the Elizabethan Englishman in Ireland Gaelic civilisation seemed primitive and even barbarous. Now in the new century with an advanced colonial policy taking root in Ireland the two civilisations confronted each other . with hostility and incomprehension. In the Gaelic lordships family, religion and the marriage structure were intertwined in a manner quite alien to the English observer and the continued existence of that way of life constituted a threat to the victorious system. Running like a minor motif through the first decades of the seventeenth century was a pre-occupation with social legislation which paralleled the efforts to achieve religious conformity. Efforts to outlaw polygamous practices among the Irish were put forward by Carew in 1611 and again at the 1634 Parliament. They were aimed at invalidating the Irish law of marriage which countenanced plurality of wives and conferred a certain legality on various types of extra-marital unions as well as allowing extensive pleadings for divorce. English law coincided with the enforcements of Tridentine ecclesiastical regulations and both were strong factors in bringing about a fundamental change in Gaelic society.

The ever pressing danger of a continental invasion was present to the Dublin administration. A number of the former leaders of the native Irish had joined the Spanish and French armies and were continually plotting to return to Ireland and win back their lands. Sir John Davies, indeed, prophesied rebellion. Yet the plain facts were that in the reign of James I the native Irish were unorganised, politically insignificant, without parliamentary representation, and further alienated from their conquerors by their adherence to a proscribed creed.

Deprived of lands, without leaders the native Irish encountered in their religion a revitalised Church and found in the Counter-Reformation clergy returning from Europe a dynamic kind of formation which adopted

Bellarmine's notion of dual loyalty as basic for political action. Gradually the cause of Catholicism became identified with that of a 'free' Ireland. 'Free' however for the Catholics of the Pale and the towns of the south meant freedom of conscience to exercise their religion. From this grew an articulate desire on the part of the Anglo-Irish, once the Stuarts established their juridical relationship as monarchs of the kingdom of Ireland, for a kingdom that would be free in the exercise of its laws, including practise of religion, while retaining allegiance to the king. In the Gaelic parts of Ireland, particularly in the north, Counter-Reformation Catholicism was accepted within the context of a 'separatist' Ireland, that is an Ireland which sought the status of a Catholic kingdom under the rule of a European prince or monarch. This aspiration was most clearly expressed in the Nine Years War and the Wild Geese were still invoking it in Flanders in the early decades of the seventeenth century. By 1603 the Counter-Reformation was firmly entrenched: among the native Irish as a vital, subversive and militant religion; among the Anglo-Irish as the most influential factor in their education.[1]

Political defeat and the opposition of the established state church rooted the Counter-Reformation more deeply into the Catholic church and the reign of James I witnessed a vigorous attempt to restore the autonomy of Catholicism by the appointment of bishops from Rome, by the restoration and reorganisation of religious orders, and by the establishment of schools. In a speech delivered to the Irish delegates who went to London in 1614 to discuss matters dealing with civil and religious liberty, James I inveighed against the activities of the Irish secular clergy, particularly those of Salamanca College, and denounced them as traitors.

Not all members of the Old Irish nobility emigrated. A number whose families had ranged with the government remained in Ireland and they were subsequently rewarded with lands in the new plantations or confirmed in possession of those they held. The Kavanaghs of Borris and Polmonty, the Dempseys of Offaly, the O'Doinns of Iregan, some of the MacMahons of Monaghan, branches of the O'Reillys in Cavan and of the O'Neills in Tyrone, the pardoned or loyalist MacCarthys and O'Briens in Munster, the Maguires, MacShanes and O'Moores became landed and in some instances were titled (James I created the title of baronet in Ireland largely to finance the Ulster plantation). Politically and socially this group had close alliances with Anglo-Irish families with whom they intermarried but unlike the Old English they possessed no tradition of free-holding. They were mainly concerned with security of land tenures and in gaining some political or adminis-trative influence. With notable exceptions like Murrough O'Brien, Lord Inchiquin and the earl of Thomond, they remained steadfast to their Catholicism and like their Old English neighbours and relatives bore the necessary fines with varying degrees of patience. As yet they were on the fringe of the struggle for constitutional rights but, in general, their aspirations were more constitutional than militant.

The Parliament of 1613–15

The legal and constitutional consolidation of the Ulster plantation brought profound unease to many in Ireland as preparations for a parliament went forward. The Ulster plantation did not involve the Old English but the heredi-tary claim put forward by the king was a dangerous precedent which might include their property eventually. The parliament summoned in 1613, the first under James I, gave them an opportunity of voicing their distrust.

Parliament in Ireland was formed on the English model but it was in many ways a pale shadow of the parent institution. It met infrequently. Between 1543 and 1613 only four parliaments were held in Ireland whereas in

England during the same period parliament met approximately twenty times with many sessions. The reign of Elizabeth in Ireland had seen the rise of a genuine opposition which became increasingly vocal over religious issues, constitutional grievances and insecurity over land titles. But the Irish parliament was not representative; it was the organ of a colony in a hostile country. In the severe crisis of the Nine Years War loyalty to the Crown and hostility to the Irish kept the Anglo-Irish firmly on the side of Elizabeth; however the forces undermining that loyalty were already at work.

With the accession of James I the Acts of Supremacy and Uniformity became a disagreeable reality in the lives of recusants. The stringent enforcement of necessary fines and forfeitures for non-conforming office-holders bore directly on the Old English who had remained Catholic and, surprisingly, the majority had. They were determined to make their dislike of the Dublin administration known, through parliament or personally to the king.

It was more than a quarter of a century since a previous parliament had sat and from 1611 onwards much searching went on among the Irish records for procedures and precedents. For months a kind of civil service panic set in because a list of names of those who sat in the previous parliament could not be found. When parliament met in May 1613 the mood of the House of Commons was spirited, bordering on the aggressive; that of the House of Lords perfunctory and non-participatory.

The House of Commons contained 132 Protestants and 100 Catholics, almost inviting an artificial opposition along lines of religious difference. The majority of the Catholic members of parliament were Old English: only eighteen native Irish sat. Resentment was immediately voiced over the forty-one new boroughs created by James which together with Trinity College returned the Protestant majority. Their real complaint, apart from the constant irritant of the recusancy fines, was that 'the knights and burgesses of the ancient shires and corporations' questioned the validity of the elections and called for an enquiry. They maintained that the numerical majority was a sham and the undignified contest over the speakership was a manifestation of their dissent. The Catholic failure to make their man, Sir John Everard, speaker was the signal for withdrawal by the Catholic opposition from the House of Commons.

In the House of Lords there was trouble over procedure. There, the Protestant majority was eventually twenty-four to twelve, the bishops of the Church of Ireland, some twenty, forming the core of the government majority. In the Lords resentment over recusancy fines was sharper and a few days after the Commons walk out, the recusant Lords followed their example. Both Houses then sent representation to James and to Lord Deputy Chichester. The continued intransigence of the recusants convinced Chichester and James's English Council that normal business would have to wait until full investigation of the recusants' grievances was carried out. The Dublin Administration stole a march however on the dissenting parliamentarians by sending their representative, the earl of Thomond to London before the official spokesmen of the recusants, Lords Mountgarret and Delvin arrived.

It is clear from the internal workings of the parliament that there was consistent manipulation and guidance by the privy councillors who formed the government front bench. Ridgeway the vice-Treasurer was in practice recognised as leader of the House with Everard, the unsuccessful candidate against Sir John Davies for the Speaker's Chair, leader of the opposition. Despite the artificial lines of opposition created by religious differences, the Irish House of Commons had a well-defined government party and an opposition which was alert, organised and watchful. The English practices of procedure including select committees and standing committees were followed. There were clear government majorities in both Houses but by October 1614 there were 108 Protestants to 102 Catholics in the Commons and in the House of Lords the government had to depend on the block vote of the bishops and on a series of *ad hoc* peers summoned rather unconstitutionally by the Dublin Administration

The legislative output of the parliament was cut short by the decision to end it somewhat abruptly in May 1615 after two sessions. Ten statutes were enacted. Seven of these, including the recognition of the king's title and prerogative and the attainder of Tyrone and Tyrconnell, were bills approved of by king and council in September 1612. As the sessions of parliament went on the House of Commons concerned itself with economic and social legislation and through committees efforts were made to redress legal and administrative abuses in the interests of landowners.

At the beginning there was a bond of sympathy between the aspirations of the recusants in both Houses but this quickly deteriorated in the atmosphere of non-attendance which marked the House of Lords. The government subterfuge of substituting *ad hoc* proxies for the absent lords only added fuel to the hostility already manifested against the Dublin Administration. The lack of corporate procedure in the day-to-day workings of the two Houses was a serious drawback. The House of Lords often remained idle and possessed no clearly defined procedure for legislative processes. A stage was reached when the Dublin Administration no longer could depend on the initiative of their majority in the House of Lords and so parliament ended.

The Parliament of 1613–15 was an important one. It marked the beginning of the conscious resistance of the Old English to the Dublin Administration which was to become more obvious in the reign of Charles I as a deliberately invoked policy to appeal to the king against his Dublin government. It also developed internally in constitutional procedure. The questioning of freedom of speech by lawyers in the Commons of both the opposition and government ranks, came from a common background of training in King's Inns and placed the whole subject of leadership of the House in better perspective. Like Perrot's parliament of 1586 it was summoned to ratify a plantation and in both parliaments the pugnacity of the recusants marked yet another stage in the conflict between the pre-planter groups and the new official class who were ruling Ireland.

Concurrently with the parliament the first regular Convocation of the church of Ireland was held in St Patrick's Cathedral. Dr James Ussher then Chancellor of St Patrick's played an influential part in its proceedings. Convocation assembled mainly to establish clearly the chief tenets of the Established Church of Ireland caught between the internal diversity of local practices and beliefs in different parts of Ireland, and the outside pressures of the Counter-Reformation Catholic Church which challenged its doctrinal position. The Irish Articles were drawn up by Ussher at Convocation. They were a combination of the Thirty Nine Articles, and the Lambeth Articles of 1595 and they showed the strong influence of Archbishop Whitgift, Elizabeth's Calvinist theologian. Though the 1615 Convocation greatly enhanced Ussher's prestige, the Irish Articles were a complex body of doctrinal statements and directives. They became in the words of the historian Dr McAdoo 'an unworkable combination of contradictory views', an opinion which is modified by Ussher's biographer, Dr R. Buick Knox.[2]

The Old English

Writers living in Europe or in England applied the term 'Irish' indiscriminately to the inhabitants of Ireland. In the middle ages 'hibernicus' had often been regarded as the equivalent of *villein* or *serf* and those of noble or important stock avoided 'hibernicus' as a description. Richard II at the end of the fourteenth century made a three-fold distinction among the population of Ireland and he adumbrated faintly the outlines of the later stereotypes in his classification of the inhabitants of Ireland as 'les irrois savages, nos enmis', the native Irish; 'les irrois rebelz', the degenerate English gone native; and 'les Englois obeissants', those by birth and by descent loyal to the Crown. By the end of the sixteenth century the term 'Irish' in English documents had assumed a quasi-legal meaning as in the phrase 'meer Irish' signifying native Irish in the Munster plantation documents, while the corresponding term 'English' became coterminous with full civic rights. It was, however, the native Irish who distinguished most clearly between Richard II's 'rebelz' and 'obeissants' in the first half of the seventeenth century by giving the name *Sean-Ghaill* (translation, Old English) to the Anglo-Irish and *Nua-Ghaill* (translation, New English) to the planters and English official class. In the estimation of the old inhabitants the terms classified the two groups into Catholics and Protestants, eventually to be recognised in the statute books at the end of the century by the legal description of protestant and papist, even as the groupings dissolved into a more homogeneous society.

Dr R. D. Edwards' discussion of the Old English in his study, 'Ireland, Elizabeth I and the Counter-Reformation' is a valuable prelude to the examination of the Old English which Dr Aidan Clarke presents between the years 1625 and 1640. Dr Edwards sees the influence of the Counter-Reformation as a determining one in defining the political as well as the religious attitudes of the Old English towards their monarch and, more acutely, towards the government in Dublin.[3] Dr Clarke is able to classify the Old English sociologically by 1625. By the reign of Charles I the Old English consisted of a nucleus of persons whose identification with it was positive and complete, and who answered in precise detail to its characteristics, together with a number of layers of persons whose identification with it was relatively less and less complete, culminating in an outer rim of persons who shaded off almost imperceptibly into other groups. This outer rim consisted of three main types. In the first place, there were the families of "degenerate English" who had become almost entirely gaelicised. In the second place there were those of Old English stock who had adopted the protestant religion without acquiring corresponding protestant interests or outlooks. In the third place, there were those of Irish extraction who associated themselves with Old English attitudes, who as one of the New English phrased it "have land, settle into an honest and fair course of life, and doubtless are well affected to the English monarchy." [4]

Dr Clarke delineates a class which emerged clearly before it joined forces with the native Irish and went down before Cromwell. There is a gap, then, between Dr Edwards' Anglo-Irish of the 1580s and Dr Clarke's Old English of the 1620s. It is a period which coincides with the spread of the Irish Counter-Reformation. During the first half of the seventeenth century the Anglo-Irish underwent several experiences which gave them an identity and a sense of belonging to a group. They lost their predominance in contemporary Irish society to the New English. They developed a political awareness of their constitutional and legal grievances. The majority of them chose post-tridentine Catholicism instead of the state religion.

For the Old English the influence of the Counter-Reformation was a quickening experience which gave both a dimension and a dynamism to the insularity of their habits. The Anglo-Irish gentry of the Pale had manifested resentment against Elizabeth's government in the 1586 parliament by refusing to pass legislation against the Jesuits. In other directions their attitudes were also appearing. They listened to the advice that their children's religion be safeguarded by sending them to Europe for education. The more influential among them withdrew their sons from Oxford and Cambridge and the practice of sending sons to the universities of Europe became common from the 1590s onwards. Prior to their departure from Ireland many of the students had acquired sufficient knowledge of the classics to enable them follow university studies in Europe. During the closing decades of the sixteenth century Latin schools were conducted in Limerick, Kilkenny, Kilmallock, Clonmel, Youghal and Waterford, mainly under Jesuit direction, and these schools sent to the continent boys trained in the classical tradition.

The decrees of the Council of Trent ordering the establishment of seminaries in all dioceses for the formation of a pious, learned, efficient and zealous clergy had important repercussions on Ireland. Colleges were founded on the continent for the education of priests for the mission in Ireland. The Irish seminary-movement deflected from Trinity College, (founded in 1591), the students for whom it was, in part, established. Generally the sons of the Catholic gentry by-passed Trinity College in favour of Louvain, Salamanca and Paris. At first the students lived a precarious existence depending on alms but towards the end of the century Irish priests, notably the Jesuit, Peter White first rector of the Irish College in Salamanca, concerned themselves with assembling the students together to live an organised collegiate life. At Douai, Bordeaux, Lisbon, Tournai, Lille, Compostella and Rome, colleges for Irish students were founded and maintained by a system of state or ecclesiastical grants.

James I was responsible for the first laws against Irish seminary priests. In June 1605 a proclamation ordering all seminary and other priests to quit Ireland before 10 December 1605 was issued, and they were forbidden to return under pain of the king's high displeasure. Six years later Lord Deputy Chichester renewed the proclamation with the addition that the sending of children overseas for education was forbidden by law, and those abroad were to return within a year under pain of confiscation of property. To no avail apparently. A report from the Irish privy council to James I in 1608 supplies the picture:

> Priests land here secretly in every port and creek of the realm, a dozen together sometimes and afterwards disperse themselves into several quarters in such sort that every town and country is full of them and most men's minds are infected with their doctrine and seditious persuasions. They have so gained the women that they are in a manner all of them absolute recusants. Children and servants are wholly taught and catechised by them, esteeming the same a sound and safe foundation of their synagogue . . . Most of the mayors and principal officers of the cities and corporate towns, and justices of the peace of this country refuse to take the oath of supremacy . . . The people in many places resort to Mass in greater multitudes both in town and country than for many years past, and if it chance that any priest, known to be factious and working, be apprehended, men and women would not stick to rescue the party . . . Such as conform and go to the state church are everywhere derided, scorned and oppressed by the multitude.

There was, then, a certain latitude in the practice of religion and after two interrupted generations the Holy See began to restore ordinary jurisdiction of bishops in England and in Ireland. In England the attempt to restore the hierarchy among a dwindling Catholic minority was abandoned in 1631. In Ireland the episcopate was organised and never lost regular continuity of succession or essential contact with the Holy See throughout the century.

The New English

One other trend in the education of the Old English at this period deserves notice. A high proportion of Irish Catholic students were admitted to Inns of Court in London. In the growing climate of uncertainty over land tenure, a knowledge of state law and its application was imperative not only for land holders but for merchants and civic families who had amassed considerable portions of real estate since the dissolution of the monasteries. If any one group in particular threatened the Old English during the first decades of the seventeenth century it was the New English.

In England the rapid development of entrepreneurial and mining activities produced a new type of land-owner, the capitalist farmer. Land and its produce was bought and sold in a competitive market and landowners began to consider their estates as a source of financial profits. The ensuing land-grabbing spread to Ireland and was a factor in attracting speculators in the various colonisation schemes.

The plantations had inserted new groupings in various regions. In Ulster the Scots-Irish became a distinct, identifiable community possessing the Scottish form of Presbyterianism. In Munster, Longford, and later Wexford, a powerful landlord-undertaker class became a permanent element in official affairs in Ireland. These were sharp legal men, possibly agents and bailiffs for larger undertakers who did not appear, and their growing prosperity was expressed in the acquisition of property. Sir James Sempill, the Scottish friend of James I, negotiated skilfully on his own behalf while ostensibly acting as middleman not only for new settlers but also for the older landholders in Carbery, County Cork. Richard Boyle later first earl of Cork, had bought up the vast Raleigh estate by 1604, and as Escheator

General had opportunities to assess the land market. George Touchet, later Lord Audley, built the town of Castlehaven, Captains Thomas Roper, Charles Coote, Francis Slingsby, Arthur Hyde and Sir John Dowdall figure in state papers as holders of minor sinecures and offices. The returns for the 1613 Parliament indicate the growing official power of the new English colonists. Though their origins were financial and legal they became by professional interests in their new properties political in the acquisition of power. They seized on every technical legality to make land available and they exploited loopholes in the law to enrich themselves and acquire more property. In Munster particularly James I allowed them to establish themselves introducing common law practice, moulding and adapting it to their own purposes. The administration in Dublin, in keeping with established Tudor policy, was composed of recent 'new English' but in the reign of James I their greed and exploitation outran the purposes of king and council in England. It was the Dublin Council, far more than James or Chichester, which pressed forward with the plantations of Longford, Westmeath, Wexford and Wicklow. It was the Dublin Council too by means of arbitrary taxations and fines which sowed rivalry among the new English class and made King James and later Charles I distrustful of giving power to the colonists. Meanwhile the new English, by their rapacity, helped to solder the Old English into a protest group.

The Old English and the Graces

Politically the threat of Catholicism in Ireland lay in its potential explosiveness in time of war, and it was the European politics of the Thirty Years War that caused the loyalties of the Old English to assume a sudden importance in the calculations of the English government. For much of the 1620s Ireland was a factor in the erratic considerations of Charles I as he strove to control both the complexities of his disintegrating foreign policy and the parliamentary challenge to his traditional prerogatives.

The appointment of Henry Cary, Lord Falkland, in 1622 coincided with King James' preoccupation with a Spanish marriage for his son. For Irish Catholics the latter meant a respite from recusancy fines. It was short-lived. The Spanish match collapsed and James left to his son who became king in 1625 the legacy of war between England and Spain. Once again Ireland became the most likely target for Spanish military operations. Moreover the bonds between Old or native Irish and Spain were strong. Rumours of conspiracies and plots for an Irish rebellion were reported faithfully by the English ambassador in Madrid from 1626 onwards.

The maintenance of the army in Ireland became of increasing concern, and for some time the Old English were in a strong bargaining position with a government desperately short of money. Technically the Old English and Irish landholders by reason of their land tenure, that of knight service-in-capite, (which involved payment of feudal dues), and by tradition were obliged to contribute 'general hostings' to the lord deputy's army. Sir John Bath acting on behalf of a group of the Old English met Falkland, the lord deputy, who had proposed introducing 'trained bands' enlisted from the Pale. Bath recommended its adoption in other provinces also but the wisdom of the scheme was queried by the government, 'for thereby we should have put arms into their hands of whose hearts we rest not well assured'.

The problem of the defence of Ireland remained. An enlarged army meant more financial spending. The emphasis switched to money-raising expedients and Charles I intimated his willingness to grant concessions out of his 'Royal grace and Bounty' in return for money. He signified his willingness to drop recusancy fines and to waive religious tests for inheritance, office-holding and legal practice. The granting of the Graces was gratifying to the Old English; it seemed to indicate that they were important and, though Catholic, entitled to special considerations. Yet preparations for a parliament to ratify the concessions fell through and when the war came to an end and the collected money was spent by Charles, the Graces were eventually repudiated.[5]

As Dr Clarke points out, if the government really trusted the Old English, it did not need to bargain concessions with them to pay for an enlarged army; it needed only to entrust them with an active part in the Irish defence. The Graces weakened the position of the Old English, exposing their vulnerability, and ultimately their helplessness.

Wentworth and a decade of crisis

By the third decade of the seventeenth century a subtle shift in the status of the Old English had taken place. Simply, the Old English had become a term of exclusion. They were now a compact group welded together by common interests and by ties of relationship. Their sense of tradition was maintained by their geographical identity with the Pale. Dublin not London was the seat of their government. The Elizabethan parliaments and that of 1613–15 had structured their constitutional awareness into a recognisable parliamentary party which could produce leadership and show resourcefulness at periods of crisis. In a sense they were political reactionaries who wished vehemently to return to a former *status quo* when they held power and the sinecures of office. Yet their religion was post-Tridentine Catholicism proscribed by a Protestant monarch whom they traditionally regarded as the ultimate source of arbitration in their affairs.

Exclusion worked both ways in the case of the Old English. If they desired to render the Dublin administration ineffectual in the 1630s it was because of their chagrin at the inclusion of their new English neighbours in the bestowal of office, a practice which had been developing since Chichester's deputyship. Increasingly political power and office had passed to the colonists and to officials directly appointed by or from England. These irritants were accentuated during the interim period between the recall of Falkland and the arrival of the new deputy when the appointed chief justices Richard Boyle, earl of Cork and Viscount Loftus, the lord chancellor, administered the country.

Unlike Falkland the lords justices were not harassed by the need to defend the country now that England was at peace. Vigorous anti-Catholic measures were applied. The Old English in particular were targets in so far as the Graces won from Charles I proved to be empty promises, and their demands for observance of various articles of the Graces, for a more equitable distribution of subsidies and for the summoning of a parliament were contemptuously set aside. Boyle in particular saw the recusants as the main threat to the government but, businesslike, he was quick to see the advantage of raising the dwindling revenue by the enforcement of recusancy fines.

It was during this brief period that the policy of plantation once again became active. It is not clear whether it was Boyle or Loftus who first mooted the confiscation of the earl of Clanricarde's estates in Connacht. By 1631 the counties of Mayo, Roscommon and Sligo were proposed to the government for a projected plantation, Sir Charles Coote being one of the advocates. The scheme was shelved until the new deputy, Sir Thomas Wentworth, would take stock.

The arrival of Wentworth in July 1633 was surrounded by distrust on the part of the Dublin Administration. Even before his arrival Wentworth had manifested a certain independence by sending his own emissary, Hopwood, to the Irish recusants to sound them on the continuation of the subsidy. It was an offer tentatively put forward and benignly received. From the beginning Wentworth planned to make his administration independent of local influence and he also wished to centralise it under his control. To effect this he had to achieve financial independence. One could argue that he was rehearsing in Ireland what he hoped to carry through eventually in England, a line of conduct which was not lost on his English opponents eventually.

Wentworth's administration of Ireland has in the past been a controverted area among historians. Lecky the great historian of eighteenth-century Ireland saw him as a great and wicked man who governed Ireland with strong and unscrupulous despotism. Trevelyan and Dr C. V. Wedgwood – in her first study of Wentworth – both saw him as a paternalistic autocrat. Irish historians in the past tended to regard Wentworth as the champion of the poor and oppressed and the opponent of graft among high government officials. Hugh O'Grady and Mary Hayden reflect this view in their respective studies. Professor Hugh Kearney imposed on himself the task of examining objectively Wentworth's administration and his study of Wentworth confirms the notion of the deputy as a great administrator concerned with augmenting the efficiency of the financial machinery at his disposal. Dr Aidan Clarke allows Wentworth to emerge gradually in his relations with both the Old English and the new settlers and he demonstrates that Wentworth in carrying out his policy of 'Thorough' ignored the political effect of his actions and alienated every influential group in the country.

The long awaited parliament was summoned in 1634. In the months since his arrival Wentworth had remained aloof but in the main he generated confidence among the Old English. He gave no hint that he would not honour the arranged programme of legislation. He had indicated that parliament would be divided into two sessions, one relating to the king's matters, the second to those of his subjects.

Wentworth's manipulation of the 1634 parliament was masterly, both in his use of Poynings Law and in his sense of timing. He had, with skill, tricked the Commons into granting him three subsidies and then in the second session he refused the Graces. The second session closed in a general atmosphere of gloom. The aloof Wentworth had revealed himself as arrogant and dictatorial, ready to pit one group against another for his own ends.

Wentworth then intimated his decision to proceed with a plantation of Connacht. This cut across the two 'darling graces' as he himself called them: the statute of Limitations and the enrolment in chancery of Old English claims to ownership in Connacht. Dr Clarke sees his scheme for the plantation of Connacht as 'the point at which the Old English and Gaelic Irish became without differentiation simply so many papists'. The earl of Clanricarde was as much Old English as any lord of the Pale and if a man of his prestige was to be subjected to the planting of his lands, who would be next?

Dissatisfaction was not confined to the Old English. In the parliament Protestant and recusant had combined to demand that the Graces be confirmed by statute. Boyle from the first had detested Wentworth, 'a most cursed man to all Ireland, and to me in particular'. Wentworth's revival of the Court of Castle Chamber caught Boyle in its toils. He was fined heavily and forced to surrender much of his church property. By 1636 the planter class, the Wilmots, the Annesleys, the Boyles, even the London Company, were antagonistic to the lord deputy.

Yet another cause of resentment was Wentworth's use of the Court of Wards and Liveries. He directed his energies to raising the revenues there by having cases of evasion or failure to secure royal permission for the property examined and by applying the rigours of wardship in the case of Catholic minors. His invocation of the Statute of Uses which he had forced through the 1634 parliament further augmented his financial projects by catching in its net those whose lands were liable to feudal dues.

Wentworth's parsimonious tactics for collecting fines were one aspect of his financial policy. Historians have conceded that Wentworth was an economic innovator, yet his movements were restricted by English interests. Anglo-Irish trade was the most important sector of Irish commerce despite the growing volume of trade between Ireland and the continent. Revenue-raising was central to the economic projects Wentworth launched but the political consequences of his actions far outweighed the economic gain he hoped for. Sheep-rearing had become extensive among the new colonists in the 1620s and the export of wool was brisk, consequently Wentworth's export duties and embargoes were resented both by the new colonists and by the merchants and traders in the Irish towns. The prohibition on the export of linen yarn, (though by it Wentworth helped to encourage the manufacture of linen at home) was resented by the Ulster planters. In general, if Wentworth had an overall economic intention it was to achieve some measure of financial stability for the Irish administration. He followed the prevailing trend of mercantilist ideas but he possessed no body of economic principles and his efforts to make Ireland pay for itself resolved into a series of economic episodes whose long term results created bitterness and hostility on the part of Irish economic interests towards England.

Wentworth has been described as one of the three great architects of seventeenth-century Absolutism, Richelieu and Olivares being the other two. For Wentworth financial stability was not an end in itself; it was the means to make possible freedom of action in other spheres and once within range of achievement, Wentworth pressed ahead with his quest for uniformity in church matters and eventual royal control in all spheres. In the years since the Convocation of 1615 the Church of Ireland had not strengthened its position. In Ulster calvanistic tendencies were reinforced by close bonds with Scottish Presbyterianism culminating in the adoption of the Covenant by Ulster settlers in the late 1630s. Wentworth's keen eyes saw serious weaknesses in the condition of the Established Church. Writing to Laud he declared that the clergy were unlearned and not held in esteem; church buildings were in disrepair; the people untutored. Church doctrine, liturgy and discipline were in a chaotic condition and Wentworth maintained that order could only be achieved by bringing doctrine and discipline in the Church of Ireland into line with that of England. But first the finances of the Church of Ireland had to be regularised. John Bramhall, bishop of Derry, was Wentworth's close adviser and together they reclaimed the revenues of the Church with a remarkable degree of success though at the cost of increased hostility from both Catholics and Ulster Scots. The Court of High Commissions was directed mainly against defaulting Protestants. Wentworth entrusted the handling of Convocation in 1634 to Archbishop Ussher and for some time he concealed his purpose of imposing the Thirty Nine Articles on the Church of Ireland. This, with Bramhall's aid, was effected and Convocation restated the place of episcopacy in the Church of Ireland and the need for a more strict conformity. By 1638 Wentworth had surmounted all obstacles to his policy of centralisation but the consensus of animosity against him among Catholics, puritans and Anglicans was remarkable in its unanimity. In July 1639 Charles I summoned Wentworth to England to support him in quelling the Scottish disorders. It was decided that parliament should be held in Ireland and in England the following year to raise money for the king's army.

Resentment is always a strong binding force where political interests are threatened. In Ireland Wentworth's policies had alienated every influential group in the country. Wentworth's application of administrative machinery like the Court of Castle Chamber, the Court of High Commission and the Court of Wards and Liveries was more than harsh; it tended towards despotic control. Parliament had been rendered subordinate to the interests of the monarch. The underlying assumption of absolutism was repudiated by all groups but particularly by the lawyers who claimed that those institutions were the instruments of common and statute laws and were not the vehicles of royal absolutism.[6]

In England the conflict emerged openly between king and parliament. In Ireland Wentworth acted as a buffer between the king and those who in the end opposed the king. The summoning of parliament in 1640 brought to the surface the constitutional aspects of that struggle. It was a short but important parliament. The involvement of the colonial settlers was much more complex than the narrowly focused attack on Wentworth – or the earl of Strafford as he now was – made it appear. As a group they had shaped common law in Ireland. King James and his officials, Lord Deputy Chichester and Sir John Davies, in their eagerness to spread common and statute law had given the colonists widespread power to mould common law according to their interpretation. Naturally they had adapted it to protect their own interests. Wentworth's treatment of the colonists cut right across their legal interests and their reaction was one of anger. The colonists were in a transitional stage. Many of them had little more in common with one another than that together they comprised the ruling settler group in Ireland. Wentworth challenged this authority and disgruntlement set in. The colonists lacked a collective history such as the Old English possessed and they borrowed the Old English constitutional tradition in the Irish parliament even as they made use of their English connections.

When the Irish parliament met in March 1640 Catholic representation stood at sixty-eight Old English and six Gaelic Irish. The Protestant majority had crept up to eighty-nine. Yet it was the Old English who defined the political situation in parliament by reason of their solidarity, their knowledge of the law and their sense of constitutional procedure. A genuine opposition coalesced between them and the puritan elements among the New English. Pym's handling of the puritans in the Irish parliament was skilful in bringing about the indictment of Strafford and the isolation of Charles I. For the Catholic members of parliament, however, the alliance put them in a false position because it was to the royal prerogative of the monarchy they had looked traditionally for protection, and it was by virtue of his royal prerogative that the king could protect them. And it was against Strafford's exercise of that royal prerogative that they had finally revolted. As for the puritans in Ireland, – drawn mainly from the ranks of the Ulster Scots – like the Presbyterians of Scotland they too would be called upon to resolve their dilemma ultimately and make the choice between king and rule of law.

It was a lawyers' parliament. Opposition was primarily concerned with the application of law. The 'petition of remonstrance' which the Irish parliament sent to the king and to the English parliament claimed the same rights for the people of Ireland as those of England. It was used in the trial of Strafford but the Irish Catholics were introducing a dangerous precedent by appealing to the English parliament in judicial affairs. The king immediately acquiesced in their demands. At last the Graces were granted. It did not, however, remove the sense of grievance.

Excited by Pym's success in the English parliament the opposition in the Irish parliament pressed further their demands. An Act of Explanation of Poynings Act was requested from the English parliament, to be followed by a series of Queries to the Judges. Wentworth's domination of an effective centralised administration resulted in a clamant demand for exclusion of that administration by defining and delineating the relationship of the Executive to the Legislature and both to the application of law.

Dr Clarke in a further study of the Old English considers that what was really at issue in the 1640 parliament was 'the relationship of the executive government to the law'; the over-riding concern was to destroy Wentworth's administration and discredit his policy.[7] The earl of Strafford was executed in May; by July the Catholic section of the Irish opposition realised that the puritans led by Parsons and Borlase were consulting the English parliament intensively. Once the common enemy had been destroyed, the alliance began to dissolve. Now their former allies were calling for the full rigour of the application of recusancy laws. So the Irish Catholics who in the spring of 1641 had allied with the puritans took arms in the autumn to defend the monarchy.

7 The Crisis of the 1640s

The stirrings of national consciousness

Among the problems which faced Gaelic society at the
beginning of the seventeenth century none was so apparent
to its writers as that of maintaining intellectual continuity
with a disappearing past. To scholars and poets who wrote
in the Irish language native culture after Kinsale and the
Flight of the Earls seemed in danger of extinction. History
and theology, two 'preservers' of culture, appear to have
been the main interests with which Irish prose writers were
concerned and the compelling need to record for the benefit
of posterity the story of Ireland's past glories and her
present tribulations occupied Irish writers whether in exile
in Europe or living a fugitive existence in Ireland. Paradoxically the decline of the bardic schools, proscribed by
law in Chichester's deputyship, released hidden springs of
poetry and mark the seventeenth century in Ireland as an
age of national literature.

Printing came late to Ireland. Its coincidence with the
burst of creative writing was important not merely for the
preservation of Gaelic culture but also for its catalystic
effect on Irish nationalism. By the seventeenth century
vernacular languages all over Europe had crystallised into
written as well as spoken forms. Governments had seized
on the potentialities of the printed vernaculars, channelling
them into government controlled uses and censoring
subversive literature which nevertheless continued to flow
In Ireland the need to make government printing available

in the Irish langauge did not escape the vigilance of the Tudor administration. Queen Elizabeth I ordered a printing press for experiments with books in Irish, chiefly of a religious or catechetical nature. With the establishment of Trinity College Dublin, Elizabeth approved the study of the Irish language and ordered the Bible to be translated into Irish and a catechism in Irish to be prepared. Though William Bedell as provost of the new university took up the project with energy, Archbishop Ussher discouraged it fearing it would foster among the Irish people an awareness of their separateness. Psychologically the project was unsympathetic to continued English policy in Ireland embodied in the legislation of the Statutes of Kilkenny.

Efforts to produce a catechism in Irish for the Established Church were countered by the Irish Franciscan friars. In Louvain where they had opened a *studium generale* they operated a printing press using an authentic Irish type which Elizabeth's printer had failed to assemble and by 1641 they had produced an Irish type face which met the approval of specialists of the Irish language. In quick succession were issued from the Franciscan printing press *Teagasg Críosdaidhe* undertaken by Giolla Bríde O hEodhasa (1611); Flaithri O Maolchonaire's *Sgathán an Chrabhaidh na hAithridhe* (1618) and Antoin Gearnon's *Parrthas an Anama* (1645), books which passed into the spiritual heritage of Gaelic-speaking Ireland for the next two centuries and bound together Catholicism and nationalism. Possibly the most important book in the first half-century of printing in Louvain was the *Acta Sanctorum Hiberniae*, known more familiarly as the *Annals of the Four Masters*, written first in Irish and then printed in Latin in 1645. It proved to be a massive compendium of information on Irish genealogical, military, social and literary history, a contemporary monument to past native culture. More pervasive in influence, however, were the works of the priest, Geoffrey Keating, poet, scholar and author of two spiritual books which long remained in use. His history, *Foras Feasa ar Éirinn* was undertaken in an effort to capture the folk history of the country before it perished. Written in limpid contemporary idiom it was a valuable contribution to printed Gaelic literature not only for its spirited refutation of Giraldus Cambrensis but for the direction it gave Irish history writing towards the conscious bias of nationalism. Printing also fixed the grammatical structure and spelling of the Irish language, (the first serious attempt at a grammar of the language was the Franciscan Bonaventure O'Hussey's *Rudimenta Grammaticae Hiberniae* printed in Louvain). In the proliferation of Irish prose and poetry in seventeenth-century Ireland there is evidence of much more than the decline of a civilisation uttering its swan-song. Wherever the printed vernacular had appeared in Europe it had been accomplished by a growing consciousness of nationalism. Ireland was no exception.

The outbreak of war and the 'Bloody Massacre'

It is clear from reports of English agents in Europe that a new militancy had crept into the attitudes of Irish exiles throughout the 1630s. To the dispossessed Irish nobility who had gone to live in Europe the recovery of their lands and the recognition of a Catholic government in Ireland became increasingly their objectives in the decade when Richelieu and Olivares were struggling for supremacy in Europe. It mattered little to Irish exiles whether it was Richelieu or Olivares who promised aid on behalf of France or Spain as long as that aid was forthcoming. Richelieu however was reluctant to give succour openly to the Irish. Spain was no less cautious but the presence of Owen Roe O'Neill as a distinguished soldier of the Spanish armies in the Netherlands gave a certain credibility to Spanish involvement in Irish affairs. In September 1639 Hopton, an English agent in Madrid, warned Secretary Windebank that an Irish conspiracy was coming to fruition involving the leading Irish exiles whom he listed by name, that of O'Neill being placed first.

Owen Roe O'Neill, nephew of Hugh O'Neill, enlisted in the service of his cousin Henry's regiment in the Spanish Netherlands shortly after the Flight of the Earls. He rapidly rose to a post of great distinction in the Spanish army while maintaining close touch with events in Ireland. When rebellion broke out in Ulster in October 1641, O'Neill corresponded with the insurgents, sending food and supplies and eventually coming himself in person in the summer of 1642. The suddenness with which rebellion broke out in Ulster threw into disarray the pattern of alliances which had been forming between Catholics and Protestants in Wentworth's Ireland. The rebellion had about it a spontaneous character comparable, as Dr Karl Bottigheimer points out, to the Edinburgh prayer-book rebellion of 1637 in that both were sparked off by local conditions. The Ulster rebellion, however, fanned out into a war lasting ten years, merging into the struggle between the king and his English parliament.[1]

Many different elements fused in the Ulster rebellion. On one level the plans of an intricate military plot were developed by a group of native Ulster nobility, notably Sir Phelim O'Neill, his brother Turlough, Lord Connor Maguire, Philip O'Reilly, Costelloe MacMahon and Sir Rory O'Moore, a Kildare landholder. The fall of Wentworth and the disintegration of his army afforded the opportunity for soliciting the help of Irish exiles on the continent and of possible re-enlistment of those soldiers whom Charles I had unwisely agreed to allow overseas to Spain. Central to the conspiracy were plans to surprise Dublin Castle together with the seizure of garrisons and forts containing arms all over the country. October 23 was fixed as the date for the general insurrection. On the previous night the plot to take Dublin Castle was revealed but the rebellion went off according to plan in Ulster.

Great fires were lit all over Ulster to act as beacons for the Irish who were everywhere hastening to enlist in the rebel armies. In the next few weeks tales of massacre and wholesale slaughter of settlers spread to England and were accepted as genuine. In a short time the myth of the 'Bloody Massacre' had assumed vast proportions and a rash of pamphlets culminated in Sir John Temple's extended pamphlet, *The Irish Rebellion* (*1646*) which became the official history of the massacre. Dr Walter D. Love has investigated the historiography of the 'Legend of the Blood Massacre' and sees it as 'a major force in perpetuating flaws in the Anglo-Irish relationship'.[2]

Even before war was declared between Charles I and his parliament, each side had played Ireland as a pawn against the other. Charles I had flirted dangerously with the disbanded officers of Wentworth's army and as late as September before the outbreak of rebellion, he was negotiating for a transfer of 8,000 men to be kept in readiness against the English parliament. On the parliamentarian side Oliver Cromwell was prominent among the group who clamoured for the military suppression of the Irish rebellion and he associated himself with the Act for Adventurers which in March 1642 placed two and a half million Irish acres confiscable by reason of the rebellion on the market for Protestant investors. This was a recognisable colonial expedient but the uniqueness of the plan embodied in the Adventurers' Act lay in its prescription that the confiscable land be taken equally out of all four provinces. By June 1642 the response to the offer was considerable and though control of the transactions eventually passed into the hands of the parliamentarians the proposed exploitation of Irish land was as attractive to Charles I as it was to those intent on seeing the king defeated. By 1644 Ireland had ceased to be an active factor in the civil war. Events in that unhappy country were lumped together in English history in what Carlyle called the 'huge blot . . . an indiscriminate darkness'.

With the outbreak of the Ulster rebellion events in Ireland moved rapidly though with a certain predictability. The immediate reaction of the Old English members of the 1640 parliament was to offer lukewarm support to the Dublin government and to send an unofficial petition to King Charles urging him to end the rebellion, not by show of force but by granting reforms. They suggested that the government of Ireland be placed in the hands of Ormond. James Butler, twelfth earl of Ormond, succeeded his grandfather in February 1633. As a minor under crown wardship he was reared a Protestant but by reason of his family background (a predominantly recusant one) and his own personality he was regarded as a natural leader among the Old English. Rather enigmatic to his contemporaries, Ormond possessed the ability to remain in the background and come forward in moments of apparent crisis. Wentworth in his last visit to Ireland arranged that Ormond would command the new army of 'Irish papists' which he was raising for King Charles. It was with Ormond, and the earl of Antrim, that the king negotiated in the summer of 1641 to recruit an army for him in Ireland, and it was Ormond who was requested by the lords justices in October to take responsibility for the defence of Dublin and the government.

Ormond's laconic preparation for war at this time is still a matter for conjecture. His hesitancy was reflected in the debacle at Julianstown where a government force sent to relieve the siege of Drogheda was heavily and ludicrously defeated. More seriously, the failure of the lords justices, Borlase and Parson, to reassure the inhabitants of the Pale that order would be maintained and that they would not be discriminated against as 'papists' led to widespread disaffection. By the beginning of 1642 the rebellion had spread to most parts of the country and, led by Lord Gormanston, the Old English of the Pale made formal alliance with the Ulstermen at the siege of Drogheda.

Militarily 1642 was a year of desultory fighting until the

arrival of Owen Roe O'Neill in July 1642 put new heart into the rebels. Politically it was a momentous year. The outbreak of civil war drew Ireland into a hostile relationship with her traditional ally, Scotland, and the landing of a Scottish army under Major-General Monro inclined the rebels towards affiliation with the king and alienated them still further from the Dublin administration. If they rejected its organs of government, it became imperative that they organise themselves and set up counter-institutions to administer the civic life of the country.

The Confederation of Kilkenny

The Confederation of Kilkenny has attracted a number of distinguished historians to its study, but the total effect is that of a brilliant beam of light casting many shadows.[3] Possibly a full synthesis of the events of this complicated decade is not yet capable of achievement until research on other aspects such as the nature and composition of the Confederate Army or the political affiliations of the New English in Ireland have reached a certain level.

In the spring of 1642 Archbishop O'Reilly at a provincial synod held in Kells proposed a form of government composed of a mixed council of laymen and clergy for the guidance of a war which the synod declared was a just one. The next step was also initiated by the clergy when a national congregation met in Kilkenny in May and was joined by prominent Catholic nobility, lawyers and merchants. Between them they set up a provisional government with a structure composed of a 'supreme council' with an elected 'general assembly', representing the parliamentary constituencies. The general assembly was to meet at least once a year and when not in session, an executive (the Supreme Council) consisting of six members from each province chosen by the General Assembly was to govern. Together they formed a single legislature having under their jurisdiction the right to determine all criminal and civil cases except those dealing with land. In descending categories there were to be provincial and county councils answerable to the Supreme Council.

In October 1642 the General Assembly, to all purposes a parliament establishing government on a regular basis, met at Kilkenny for the first time. They styled themselves 'the Confederate Catholics of Ireland' and they bound themselves individually by an oath of association pledging under pain of excommunication to restore 'the right of the Church, the prerogatives of the Crown and the liberties of the nation'. They adopted the words 'Pro Deo, pro rege, pro patria Hibernia unanimis', for the Confederate seal, a motto capable of as many shades of interpretation as there were groupings in the Confederation.

Ostensibly the Confederation symbolised the unity of the kingdom and the juridical relationship between the kingdom and its monarch was indeed a bond of loyalty between the different groupings represented in the Confederation. But the groupings were diverse and the structure too cumbersome for a time of war. Their constitutional sense of finesse stood the Old English in good stead and within a relatively short period they dominated the sittings of the Council. The Catholic hierarchy which replaced the Protestant bishops as representatives in the quasi-parliament, (the Confederation), were a distinct group by reason of their continental counter-reformation training, their order of priorities and the talent at their disposal. The Old or native Irish though involved in confederacy levels of government lacked constitutional experience and unlike the Old English their sense of urgency about guarantee of land tenure was somewhat blunted by actual loss of lands. They were in the early stages a group who could swing right to the moderate Old English royalist side or alternatively they were capable of attaching themselves to a particular cause if its advocates were at all persuasive. Polarisation occurred rather unexpectedly around the persons of the papal representatives, Scarampi and Rinuccini who together with Owen Roe O'Neill wrested domination of the Confederation away from the Old English and from the civic merchant and lawyer elements who were primarily concerned with the land settlement aspects, and placed the Catholic religion with accompanying guarantees as the major concern of the war.

Progress of the War

The war, however, did not become a religious war. It was a war where conflict of aims and issues made strategic coherence impossible. Sir Phelim O'Neill had stepped down in favour of his cousin Owen Roe O'Neill as commander of the Ulster forces. The unconcealed hostility and rivalry between Owen Roe and Colonel Thomas Preston, brother of Lord Gormanston who had also returned from service in Flanders to participate in the Irish struggle made concerted action practically impossible, and to Preston was given command of the Confederate forces in Leinster. O'Neill, after assuming leadership, disciplined the ragged army which he gradually moulded into an effective and orderly fighting force. It was a daunting task in view of the efficient and united forces of Leslie and Monro and the slow climb to the victory of Benburb (1646) was strewn with frustrations and disappointments. Meanwhile King Charles intimated to Ormond that he was prepared to treat with his Irish confederate subjects in January 1643. A few months later he commissioned Ormond to arrange a cessation of arms for at least one year. With the opening of negotiations between Charles and the Confederate Catholics of Ireland a distinct phase is discernible, not merely in the Irish war but in the civil war between Charles and his parliament. It was inconceivable that the king, indispensable symbol of state authority could be in rebellion yet how explain that His Majesty was leading an army against one raised by parliament's command and soliciting an Irish army composed of papists, delinquents and others ill-affected?

Once negotiations with the king came to be admitted within the Confederates' terms of reference Protestant royalism asserted itself. Ormond was appointed Lord Lieutenant late in 1643 and the king entrusted to him negotiations for a settlement with the Confederates. He found himself caught between the competing claims of Catholic and Protestant interests and his own firm adherence to Protestantism made him an uncompromising negotiator. The dreary succession of attempted treaties for the next few years, Glamorgan's secret mission, the queen's treaty (sometimes known as the Roman treaty) and finally Ormond's negotiated peace in 1646 illustrate the growing disharmony between the different groups. Scarampi was replaced by Rinuccini as fully accredited nuncio in October 1645 to the gratification of the Confederates. A sincere but impetuous man Rinuccini plunged into a situation which required the utmost tact and diplomacy and shattered the unity of the Confederation. Almost immediately he identified his mission with that of O'Neill and to him gravitated those who distrusted Ormond and proclaimed zeal for the Catholic religion.

It was a period of marked contrasts in the war situation. The surrender of King Charles to his Scots and their relinquishing of him to the English parliament in 1646 resolved nothing for the Irish. The same year saw the victories of Confederate armies in the north and north-west of Ireland, Benburb (1646) being the most spectacular. Yet O'Neill abandoned his strategic attack on Monro's forces and marched south to Rinuccini who in August condemned the Ormond Peace Treaty at a synod. This was followed by the symbolic, almost biblical, entry of O'Neill and his army in triumph into Kilkenny accompanied by the nuncio. Together they proceeded to depose and imprison the Supreme Council who had ratified the treaty. Rinuccini assumed control of the interim council. Preston, intimidated at first by the nuncio's strictures, agreed to attack Dublin then held by Ormond in conjunction with O'Neill. This concerted action was abandoned when both generals disagreed, O'Neill withdrawing his troops while Preston vacillated between Ormond and the nuncio.

The year 1647 saw many changes of heart. By the New Year there was a growing reaction to the nuncio's action. He himself felt it and released the imprisoned members of the Supreme Council. The General Assembly met in January and rejected the Ormond Peace emphatically but the Confederates were split. Historians have classified the divided parties into 'Ormondists' and 'Nuncioists'. In fact the realities of the situation made a clear-cut division impossible. For example the holders of former ecclesiastical property – and this included the influential merchant group – were unhappy with the nuncio's uncompromising demands for religion. Again until further research makes it clear, it is difficult to determine the political and economic objectives of the Ulster and native Irish Confederates at this time. The Old English Confederates, on the other hand, were unwilling to abandon negotiations with Ormond. Ormond's decision to hand over the keys of Dublin to the representatives of the English parliament signified his intransigence towards the nuncio. In July he left Ireland having surrendered his garrisons and transferred Dublin to the parliamentary forces. After his departure internal hostilities among the Confederates worsened. Their armies fared badly and the decision of the Eighth General Assembly in November 1647 to send envoys to Rome and France for help was offset by the wranglings and divisions in the Assembly. The Old English Confederates favoured a truce with Inchiquin, victorious leader of the parliamentarian forces in Munster. The Nuncio, in a vain effort to regain control of the Supreme Council excommunicated those who associated themselves with the Inchiquin Truce.

O'Neill's authority, solidly in support of the nuncio, was set aside. It was then that Inchiquin changed sides and supported the king.

Inchiquin's alliance with the Royalists and with Ormond in April 1648 can be explained in terms of self-interest. His army was a different matter. One large section remained loyal to their leader and less enthusiastically served the king. The other section adhered to the Parliament and either defected to the Dublin garrison of Michael Jones or joined the Parliament's navy patrolling the southern coast of Ireland. The civil war had finally penetrated Ireland.

In September 1648 Ormond arrived back in Ireland and completed a treaty with the Confederates which differed little from the 1646 one. Rinuccini left Ireland in February 1649 having manifested his displeasure with the Treaty. The Confederacy was replaced by a central command of twelve commissioners under Ormond. O'Neill preferred to go his own way and relying on former continental bonds with the leaders of the Ulster Scots armies, made overtures to them, not without success. Michael Jones too refused Ormond's invitation to ally with him and preferred to hold Dublin and Ormond's troops at bay until he defeated them resoundingly at the Battle of Rathmines in August 1649. Cromwell landed at Ringsend in Dublin a fortnight later.

Cromwell's campaign in Ireland was swift, terrible and decisive. O'Neill's death in November 1649 after the Sack of Drogheda removed the only commander who would have been a rallying point against Cromwell, though Cromwell and his 3,000 Ironsides were formidable in their discipline, military experience and in the genius of the commander. Cromwell's campaign was technically an invasion and his army was the avenging one of the victorious Republic which had executed King Charles and was now intent on winning political and religious security throughout the state. A subdued Ireland was essential to the

Surat
Calcutta
Bombay
Madras

Gambia
Gold Coast

Hudson's Bay
Maryland
New England
New York
Virginia
Pennsylvania
Bermuda
Bahama
Jamaica
Honduras
Barbados

English colonial expansion in seventeenth century

economic development of the Republic which looked westward to colonial extension. Cromwell was conscious of this when he wrote his 'Declaration of the Lord Lieutenant of Ireland, For the Undeceiving of Deluded and Seduced People'.[4]

Dr Bonn draws the conclusion: 'It was necessary therefore to create an order of circumstances whereby it would no longer be permitted to prejudice the international situation of England and protestantism, nor that it would imperil English liberty and the life of its adherents which could only be achieved if England was strong enough in Ireland to make any hostile action impossible both from external powers and from the Irish themselves.'[5]

When Cromwell departed from Ireland in May 1650 he left behind him a country whose final conquest was certain though his successor, Ireton, took another two years to complete it. Cromwell with military precision had moved from one vantage point to another. He subdued Ulster, then moved south to Wexford and New Ross. He besieged Waterford and Cork; Youghal and Kinsale ceded to him. Kilkenny was his by March and Clonmel after sturdy fighting, his by May. To Ireton was left the task of taking Limerick, Galway and a few isolated strongholds in Ulster. Ireland was abandoned to the Republic first by Charles Stuart, son of the executed king when he repudiated the Ormond Treaty with the Confederates in August 1650, and then by Ormond himself who left Ireland in December 1650 to join Charles Stuart. By the summer of 1652 Ireland was reduced to the status of a conquered colony and preparations were made for a vast settlement of the country.

8   Change and Restoration

The Cromwellian plantation

By 1653 even Inishbofin off the coast of Connemara had
been taken by the Cromwellians and famine and pestilence
stalked the land. Starvation was general, the wolves coming right down into the towns and carrying off people
from outlying houses. Ludlow marching from Nenagh to
Portumna tells the story in his *Memoirs* of how his advance
guard captured two rebels and having killed one on the
spot brought the second to Ludlow. Ludlow with heavy
military humour interrogated him and said: 'Have you a
mind to be hanged?'; whereupon the poor wretch
stammered 'If you please', raising a general laugh at his own
expense. Like Scotland in the Cromwellian decade the
embodying of Ireland with England was 'as when the poor
bird is embodied into the hawk that hath eaten it up'.
Though power rested nominally with the English House of
Commons, in reality it was the army who sustained
Cromwell's republic.

'The origins of the concept of the Cromwellian plantation', remarks Goblet its greatest historian, 'are no less
complex than those politics of which it was destined, in the
mind of the government, to assure the final triumph.'[1]
Despite biblical overtones of chastisement in the thinking
surrounding the Cromwellian Settlement, economic preoccupations in the end prevailed in this 'Grand Design'.
Cromwell's commissioners discovered that their main task
was to settle the outstanding accounts of the soldiers and

officers and to pay those who had 'adventured' money in 1642 and were now clamouring to be recompensed. The 1642 Adventurers Act had pledged two and a half million Irish acres to meet the cost of the Irish war. This was the rub. The solution was set out in the Act for Settling Ireland which was passed in the English Parliament in August 1652.

This act excluded from pardon 1) such as at any time prior to November 1642 (the first sitting of the General Assembly) advised or promoted rebellion, murders or massacres in Ireland; 2) by name the earls of Ormond, Castlehaven, Clanricard, Fingal, Roscommon and West-meath, and the baron of Inchiquin; 3) the principals and accessories since October 1641. The ordinance went on to admit of pardon upon conditions of qualifications four other classes of people: a) such as not falling within the unpardonable groups bore arms against the Common-wealth, should suffer banishment and loss of two third of their estates (the Confederate army); b) such as not falling within the said groups, aided in the rebellion, should be pardoned with their lives but forfeit two thirds of their estates and receive value elsewhere (the landowners favourable to the Confederates); c) all Roman Catholics in Ireland between October 1641 and March 1650 and did not manifest constant good affection should forfeit one fifth of their lands; d) all other persons not possessed of real or personal property to the value of £10 should lay down arms and be pardoned.

Gardiner the English historian estimated that if the law were rigorously enforced, 10,000 would be found guilty. This however was not the case. In September 1653 the English Parliament appointed Connacht as the place of transportation whither those convicted were to transport themselves before May of the following year. The ordin-ance rested for a year while the surveys were being carried out.

The notion of a projected plantation in Connacht at

which Wentworth had been working most likely suggested to the English Council of State and their commissioners for the affairs of Ireland, the idea of moving out of Leinster, Ulster and Munster (except Clare) into Connacht and Clare the convicted landowners and occupying tenants of the forfeited lands, their respective families and their followers. Goblet suggests that the plan for the Cromwellian Settlement bears the marks of administrative and military thinking deeply affected by geographical considerations. A proposal by the army officers to the commissioners of Ireland to constitute the south-east as a 'Pale' peopled exclusively with English who would guard the passage of the Boyne and Barrow and so form a complete frontier was made as early as December 1651. In June 1652 Connacht was designated the place of deportation and would constitute another type of 'Pale', an Irish one, isolated by the Shannon. The countryside between those two regions would be peopled with a mixed population and the ten counties listed for the use of the colonists in the first section of the 1653 Act would form a large band of territories stretching diagonally from north-east to the south-west of Ireland. It was a project conceived at a time when the notion of 'native reservation' was appearing in colonial policy across the sea.

Winter was chosen as the time of exodus, both to prevent any applications for the harvest of 1654 and to allow the new settlers to assume ownership at a slack period. Much of the transplantation had been completed by July 1654. About 44,000 people with foodstuffs and farm animals had moved across the Shannon. Yet the unhappy exodus was accomplished with considerable care and undoubted success; no record of pestilence or accident exists. A census taken in 1659 reveals that it was not a transportation of the entire native population; there remained behind a large body of Irish labourers. As in the Ulster plantation there remained former occupiers of the land who formed themselves into bands of brigands and found their way into state reports as a constant irritant under the name, 'Tories'.

The Cromwellian Settlement was based upon three Surveys: the Gross Survey, the Civil Survey and the Down Survey of Sir William Petty. As we have seen the ancient processes by law for surveying forfeited lands were by inquisition out of chancery or exchequer on the precedents established by the Desmond surveys of Elizabeth, and by commission under the great seal as used under James I in Ulster. The second mode was adopted by the Cromwellian commissioners Fleetwood, Ludlow, Corbett and Jones who were given plenipotentiary powers to carry out the settlement in June 1653. Under mounting pressure of demand the Gross Survey had been hastily assembled but was abandoned even before being completed because of faulty surveying. It was then decided to make a survey of the country founded upon authentic information of the old inhabitants as a preliminary to mapping. Twenty-seven counties were to be surveyed; Wentworth's 1636 survey being used for Clare, Galway, Mayo, Sligo and Roscommon. The barony was selected as territorial basis for the survey which was made under oath in courts of survey. Each barony survey opens with a description of its bounds and soil, concluding with an account of the parishes, manors and castles within the barony, some indication of the boundaries of parishes and a statement of tithes due. The Civil Survey was then a manuscript taken down by deposition and what emerges is the 'old inhabitants' survey of their country, of its place names (rendered phonetically into the English of the time), ancient forms of tenure, land measurements and divisions. It did not confine itself to being a survey of forfeited lands but became a description of Ireland, a geography of its mountains, rivers and roads, a record of ownership and title to lands. In short a kind of Doomsday Book of seventeenth-century Ireland.

The Civil Survey was an essential preliminary to the skilled Down Survey undertaken by Sir William Petty who with the Surveyor General, Benjamin Worsley, was responsible for the admeasurement and mapping of the transportation scheme. William Petty who erupted on the Irish scene towards the end of 1652 was then thirty years of age, an engaging adventurer with very real pretensions to scientific learning and methodology. He was immediately attracted to the challenge presented by the project of mapping for a large-scale settlement and offered to complete a mapped survey of the country within thirteen months. The army accepted his offer and Dr Petty with his team of soldiers whom he trained personally to do fieldwork completed the Survey maps in record time. Handsomely recompensed both in money and land Petty spent the rest of his life perfecting and expanding his maps of Ireland. Petty's maps were the work of an inspired geographer and though they did not escape the criticism and grumbling of the army, the methods he used and his subsequent account of the process make the Down Survey one of the most interesting contributions to the history of cartography.

After the Cromwellian Plantation a new Ireland took shape. The successful removal of Catholic landowners and well-to-do merchants and tenants either by transportation or emigration placed the sources of wealth and power into the hands of Protestant colonists. Within the important decade of the Restoration Parliament, property and political power passed from the older inhabitants into the possession of the colonists, and in particular to the 'Cromwellian interest'. The old town corporations which had been controlled by Old English recusants now passed out of their hands; those who remained had little power or influence. Civic life, political authority and landownership had passed finally into the hands of colonial settlers. The long span of colonisation begun with the plantation of

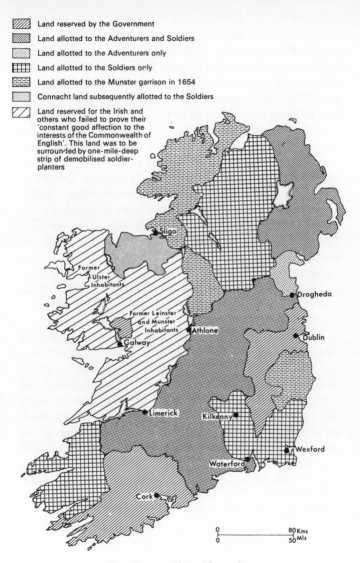

Land reserved by the Government

Land allotted to the Adventurers and Soldiers

Land allotted to the Adventurers only

Land allotted to the Soldiers only

Land allotted to the Munster garrison in 1654

Connacht land subsequently allotted to the Soldiers

Land reserved for the Irish and others who failed to prove their 'constant good affection to the interests of the Commonwealth of English'. This land was to be surrounded by one-mile-deep strip of demobilised soldier-planters

Former Ulster Inhabitants

Former Leinster and Munster Inhabitants

Sligo

Drogheda

Galway

Athlone

Dublin

Limerick

Kilkenny

Wexford

Waterford

Cork

0   80 Kms
0   50 Mls

The Cromwellian Plantation

Leix and Offaly was accomplished by the Cromwellian Confiscation as it was modified finally in the Williamite Settlement and with the Restoration of Charles II the new Cromwellian proprietors took their place among the 'New English' of the seventeenth century at the apex of the social and political hierarchies in Ireland.

In the countryside the changes brought about by the new owners were part of a pattern previously established. An acute labour shortage occurred, partly from disease and famine, and partly from mass-emigration. Until well into the Restoration decade the new farms fared badly. The settlers favoured tillage and enclosure became common though in the 1680s open land was still extensive. The potato assumed popularity rapidly, and mixed vegetable gardening close to the towns began to appear. Apple orchards were cultivated notably in Kilkenny, Tipperary and Armagh. New clovers were introduced into grasslands and stud-farming took firm root among the occupations of the new landowners.

The greatest change in the landscape, however, was the clearance of the forests accompanied in a number of places by the belching fires of furnaces and forges. The use of charcoal for iron-smelting meant ceaseless depredations on wood-stocks. Boyle's furnaces on the Blackwater were for a time the main centre of the Irish iron-industry until local resources were exhausted towards the end of the century. Other smelting areas such as the Lagan valley near Belfast and around Castlecomer in County Kilkenny had similar life-spans. As Orme points out 'the indiscriminate rape of the woodlands for charcoal had a more significant long-term effect on the landscape than the transitory existence of furnaces and forges'.[2]

The Restoration of Charles II

To endeavour to apply the term 'Restoration' to Ireland after 1660 is misleading. Certainly the monarchy was restored as were the privy council, judicature and parliamentary machinery. The Irish nobility led by Ormond were to enjoy their own again but like Scotland it was those lords who had supported the Cromwellian regime who were destined to rule. Lord Broghill and Sir Charles Coote found that service under the Commonwealth was not a liability.

The exiled Charles II had gained his throne through British sentiment. General George Monck, commander-in-chief of the army in Scotland brought Charles Stuart back by constitutional means of a freely elected Parliament. In Ireland the army officers ranged themselves on his side and shortly after Monck's call to the Irish officers to join him, Dublin Castle was seized through a minor coup involving Sir Theophilus Jones and a group of fellow officers and an invitation was issued to Sir Charles Coote and Lord Broghill to come to Dublin as 'advisers'. Meanwhile Henry Cromwell, a son of Oliver, who had succeeded Fleetwood as deputy of Ireland, quietly resigned his post even before his brother Richard was deposed by the Rump of the Long Parliament in May 1659. The restoration of Charles II in Ireland was accordingly accomplished by the 'new interest'. A convention met in Dublin roughly on the lines of Wentworth's boroughs nearly twenty years before. There it was agreed that the king should be restored. Both the Irish Convention and the Irish army joined Monck in demanding that the Rump Parliament readmit the members it expelled in 1649, so establishing a majority in favour of the Restoration. In such a manner the Long Parliament finally dissolved itself and a Convention, on the Irish model, opened negotiations with Charles II. Shortly afterwards the Restoration was proclaimed in England, then in Ireland. 'I stood in the Strand', wrote Evelyn in his diary, 'and beheld it, and blessed God'. Bagwell the Irish historian of Tudor and Stuart Ireland delivers a memorable passage on the Restoration of Charles II.

Charles II wily, untrustworthy and well endowed with a quick brain and speech was plausible and inventive. Inured from youth to compromise he was not greatly moved by principles. He was not religious by temperament but possibly inclined to tolerance by his indolent habits and early experiences. He was not a great monarch. He was cool, he kept his nerve and his throne.

With some show of speed the old framework of government in Ireland was restored. A Privy Council of thirty-four members was re-established with Sir Philip Mainwaring, one of Wentworth's officials in 1634 present after twenty years of poverty and some of imprisonment. Sir Charles Coote was reinstated as president of Connacht, Lord Broghill for Munster. Other lesser appointments were filled like Sir James Barry as Lord Chief Justice; Sir William Domville as Attorney General; Arthur Annesley, vice-treasurer, later to be created earl of Anglesey. Monck was appointed lord lieutenant but acquired a deputy, the cranky Lord Roboartes.

'The first thing a king should learn' wrote Temple in his *Essay* (1668) 'is to say no, so resolutely as never to be asked twice, nor once importunately!' Nowhere was Charles II's inability to say no so evident as in the events leading to the Court of Claims and the Act of Explanation. The adventurers and soldiers occupied the best part of Ireland and by the proclamation of Charles II they were confirmed in their possessions until the king with the advice of the English or Irish parliament should 'further order, or that they be legally evicted by due course of law'. But Charles II was also bound by the 1642 Adventurers Act which pledged two and a half million of Irish acres for the cost of the war. It was already obvious from the manner of the Restoration in Ireland that the Cromwellian interest was dominant. Subsequent to the proclamation a Declaration of Indulgence was hammered out leaving the Adventurers and soldiers more or less in possession of their occupied lands while making some provision for Irish proprietors who were not engaged in the rebellion or who had served the king abroad. Despite Clarendon's scathing remark that 'the miserable Irish alone had no part in contributing to H.M's happiness', Charles was protective towards his Irish supporters. All the land possessed by the Adventurers 7 May 1659 was secured to them; those whose claims had not been fully satisfied were to have the deficiency made good out of territory assigned to them as a body but not yet distributed. Church lands were excepted. Innocent Papists, Ensignmen (those who had followed the king abroad), eighteen special nominees of the king, the peers Westmeath, Clanricard, Clancarty, Mountgarret, Taafe were to be restored; Ormond and his wife were rewarded, and Inchiquin was rumoured to have turned papist as well as royalist.

The Declaration needed legal sanction of parliament and in May 1661 Parliament opened ceremoniously in Chichester House, Sir Audley Mervyn being elected speaker. Members were returned from thirty-two counties, 108 boroughs and from Trinity College, Dublin. The boroughs were divided into four types: freeman, corporation, potwalloper and manor, depending on the nature of the franchise. Though their role was still in process of definition, with the Restoration parliamentary returns, there existed the machinery which kept the Ascendancy in political control for the following century. In all 339 persons sat in parliament during its settings. The members were Protestant and continuance of its Protestant character was assured in the Commons by having the oaths of supremacy and allegiance administered to all members. Among the members their relationship with the late king and his conflict with parliament was one kind of division but much more important to the superficial unity of the whole body was their signified opposition to the late Irish rebellion. It was a parliament whose mood was kept constantly in minor key and where the larger issues were played down. One reason for that was that much business was arranged away from parliament through the king and Ormond who was appointed viceroy in 1662.

Parliament sat from May 1661 until August 1666. At first it was dominated by the 'new' or Cromwellian interest and the tone was set by Jeremy Taylor's opening sermon on 'Rebellion – the son of witchcraft'. Though the main interest of all the members centred on the legislation surrounding the Declaration of Charles, tensions remained concealed until 1663 when the House of Commons protested once the implications of the Act of Settlement passed the previous year became clear. Dissatisfaction with the Act of Settlement which constituted a threat not only to the Cromwellian interest but to the older Protestant interest led to the establishment of a Court of Claims and the appointment of Commissioners to examine the cases of 'Innocents'. Once again Charles and Ormond had adroitly channelled business into extra-parliamentary areas.

Among the seven commissioners appointed, Sir Winston Churchill has left a record of his impressions. After the first day's sitting of the Court of Claims two claimants were declared innocent, and one guilty. By the expiration date of the Court only one-sixth of the applicants had been heard and 800,000 acres had been restored. Discontent was rife in the House of Commons and the news that Lord Antrim, King Charles' Catholic friend, was restored by letter of the king increased the alarm, which culminated in the abortive Castle Plot against Ormond. Sir William Domville, the Attorney General, held that over a million acres of profitable land had been set out to the Adventurers and soldiers as unprofitable and that there were immense quantities of concealed land. It was not without foundation though Ormond remarked that 'there must be new discoveries made of a new Ireland, for the old will not serve to satisfy these engagements. It remains then to determine which party must suffer in the default of means to satisfy all; or whether both must be proportionately lesser'.

Attempts to have a Bill of Explanation passed which would modify the Act of Settlement were resisted until 1665 when it passed without a division mainly through Ormond's efforts. Churchill described the fierce opposition that took place in the House of Commons until dusk fell, 'the members confronting each other with swords half-drawn and with words sharper than they'. He attributed the final triumph to Ormond who 'by an eloquence peculiar to himself seemingly unconcerned but certainly extempore, so charmed their fears and jealousies that they who were most displeased with the Bill were yet so pleased with the overtures he had made them that when it came to pass it had only one negative'.

The emergence of Ormond again at the Restoration period as a leader was significant. Though he was willing to listen and even to take advice from men like the earl of Orrery (Broghill) the unquestionable authority of Ormond, his control of parliament, his personality which had become more expansive with the royal restoration made him par excellence a moving equilibrium in the fluid politics of restoration Dublin.

Charles II had concluded his speech to the Convention 27 July 1660 with the words: 'I hope I need say nothing of Ireland, and that they alone shall not be without the benefit of my mercy. They have showed much affection to me abroad, and you will have a care of my honour and of what I promised them. . . . ' According to Daniel O'Neale, one of Charles' Irish friends in exile, the Act of Settlement 'put the poor Irish in a fair way of extirpation'. Petty considered the land settlement as the chief source of division in a divided country. Dr Simms, historian of the Williamite Settlement, considers that the restoration settlement was regarded by Irish Catholics as a breach of faith, and that they were prepared to upset it at the first opportunity.

Land was uppermost as a political concern for the rest of Charles' reign. Though the Catholic position continued to improve due to the king's good will and the efforts of Richard Talbot, friend of James duke of York, yet the Protestant ascendancy was established. By the end of Charles' reign most of Ulster, Leinster and Munster was held by Protestant landowners. Galway alone was predominantly Catholic in landownership. Yet there remained a deep-seated dread of a Catholic revival among the landholders, an apprehension not allayed by the conversion to Catholicism of James, duke of York.

The Churches in Restoration Ireland

The Restoration Parliament was overwhelmingly Church of Ireland in religious complexion. Primate Bramhall wrote to Secretary Nicholas: 'At our first sitting we had troubles in both Houses of Parliament, but by good managements they are calmed . . . we have established the liturgy, doctrines and disciplines of the Church. We have condemned the Covenant engagement.' Among the first acts of Charles II was the re-establishment of the hierarchy in the Established Church. Eight Irish bishops had survived the Commonwealth. They were John Bramhall (Derry), Henry Jones (Clogher), Henry Leslie (Down), John Leslie (Raphoe), Robert Maxwell (Kilmore), Griffith Williams (Ossory), Thomas Fulwar (Ardfert) and William Baylie (Clonfert). Bishop Jones had acted as Scout Master General to Cromwell and the restored Church was to be one which would not offend Presbyterian susceptibilities unduly. Bramhall was appointed Primate in 1661; an attractive and able character, he died suddenly in 1663.

By the Declaration issued by Charles II in 1660 and later incorporated into the Act of Settlement all lands held by the Church in 1641 were to be restored, as well as all lands held on lease from the bishops by persons who had forfeited them to the Crown. Tithes were to be restored and a glebe to be provided in every parish. From the vantage point of endowment the Restoration Settlement seemed satisfactory. Bramhall quickly filled up the depleted ranks of the bishops and in St Patrick's Cathedral two archbishops and ten bishops were consecrated together. It was at this memorable ceremony that Jeremy Taylor, the Restoration Divine, was consecrated bishop of Down and Connor where his troubles with the unruly Presbyterians clouded his serene spirit and hastened his death in 1667.

Primate Bramhall too was having his troubles. He was a sturdy upholder of royal supremacy and subscribed to the notion of Catholicity of the Churches of England and Ireland. He believed in comprehension and desired a broad-based institutional church which would include Calvinists and Armenians. Though he detested the papacy he was tolerant towards Irish Catholics and no shadow of persecution arose during his short ministry. He rebuilt churches, showed himself an enemy of non-resistance and, learned himself, he tried to procure a more learned clergy. The Established Church, however, did not maintain its hopeful beginnings. The *State Memo* of 1666 throws light on the situation. Protestant bishoprics were nearly equal in size of those of England and their revenue was about two-thirds of the English arrangement. There were numerous deaneries and chapters in Ireland but few cathedrals in repair. There were not more than 500 preachers and the parishes in Ireland were twice or thrice as large as in England with three, four or five combined to make a living for a minister. The impropriate tithes were many. In 1668 Primate Margetson's salary was £3,500 but Clonfert was only £400 and Kildare £200. The clergy of the Church of Ireland in Connacht received sums ranging from 40/– to 16/– a year. Ill-paid, scattered, loosely organised and depressed those clergy had to encounter the highly organised Roman Church which after the arrival of Archbishop Oliver Plunket and the Synod of 1666 became a disciplined Church.

It was understandable that the religious unity which the

Restoration government tried to attain would be shaken by any determined coalition. In 1661 the government tried to hinder meetings of Papists, Presbyterians, Independents, Anabaptists and Quakers who were joined together as the common enemies of the State as of the Church.[3] Petty estimated that the population of Ireland in 1672 was around 1,200,000; by the end of the reign of Charles the population was 1,300,000. The population of Dublin numbered about 32,000 of whom the majority were Church of Ireland. Of the remainder Petty reckoned that there were 800,000 Roman Catholics in 1672 and the remaining 400,000 were Protestants in the wide sense. At least half of that number were Presbyterians in Ulster and among the remainder were Quakers, Anabaptists and other sects.

For the Quakers Restoration Ireland was their most creative period in the country. As a sect they were hard-pressed on every side. Their doctrine of 'Inner Light' held with fervour by Burrough during his imprisonment in Dublin under Henry Cromwell and passed on to his followers led to persecution because of the way of life advocated. The clergy opposed them because of their assertion of the non-necessity of human intermediaries between God and man, and because they declared the Gospels to be free and that no-one had a right to earn money by preaching. The government opposed them because of non-juring. The ruling class were annoyed by their lack of respect and their custom of keeping their hats on always. Traders and merchants resented their sturdy business sense.

The visit of George Fox in 1669 began the regular keeping of records which were sustained for over a century. From these records it would seem that there were between 600 and 700 families of Quakers in Ireland in the 1680s. About half of these came from the North of England and about one-third were concentrated in or around Dublin with strong centres in Queen's County and Wicklow. In Dublin Anthony Sharp enjoyed a good reputation in the city and became a master weaver without taking the oath, eventually being elected an alderman of the city. He was mainly responsible for the new charter under James II. Admiral Penn, father of William the founder of Pennsylvania, was an adventurer who received a grant of 12,141 acres in Cork. James, duke of York was a personal friend of William Penn and guaranteed protection to the Irish Quakers. When king he granted them freedom of conscience and they were placed in Jacobite corporations. The Restoration Church however continued to be hostile to them because of the refusal of the Quakers to pay tithes.

The Catholic Church

Apart from the Presbyterians, the Roman Catholics were the religious group who offered the most serious threat to the unity of the Established Church. The history of Catholicism in the Restoration period was one of imperceptible growth. The action of the counter-reformation was a continuous one: continuity being achieved by a hierarchy which never, in an official sense, needed to be restored. During the Protectorate a penal situation had existed: priests were banished, religious houses closed and for a brief period imprisonment and death were the order of the day.

Charles II was well-disposed towards his Catholic subjects but he was obliged to come to terms with the Cromwellian puritans who dominated the settlement. It was not long before remonstrances got under way. The Quakers of London produced an *Apologia* protesting their plight and the Presbyterians also petitioned. Ormond, newly appointed as lord lieutenant went to some trouble to elicit a declaration of loyalty from Irish Catholics. He chose Peter Walsh, a learned Franciscan, to draw up the remonstrance.

The Irish Remonstrance of Peter Walsh nearly caused a schism in the Irish Church. It denied in effect indirect papal power in temporal affairs. Rebellion was judged unlawful and any papal or foreign interference with the Crown of Charles II was rejected. It was presented to Charles II early in 1662 and Charles demurred because it was unsigned. This posed problems for Walsh. Catholic clergy were filtering back to Ireland and some of them had long memories of Walsh's anti-nuncio stand in the Confederate wars. He succeeded in subscribing twenty-four Irish clergy in London including the ambitious Bishop Oliver Darcy but his own order in Louvain was uneasy and prevailed on the University of Louvain to censure Walsh's Remonstrance as being offensive to papal dignity. Walsh replied with a pamphlet, *The more Ample Account*, published in London 1662, which was a political tract, absolutist in tone. Meanwhile Rome was anxious to build up cordial relations with Charles II and was seriously embarrassed by Walsh's persistence in drawing attention to the indirect power of the papacy.

Gradually the Irish Catholic clergy withdrew into two groups, Remonstrants and Anti-remonstrants, the latter being in the majority. Efforts were made to draw up alternative remonstrances to no avail and when Ormond returned in September 1665 with the Act of Explanation from London, the hopes of Catholic landowners were dashed. Walsh now demanded a general meeting of the Irish clergy which finally took place in June 1666 in Dublin.

Ormond's efforts to influence the proceedings together with Walsh's aggressive tactics turned the clergy against him. They drew up an alternative Act of Recognition which Ormond rejected. This congregation has been called the Synod of 1666, significant both for the publicity with which it was held in Dublin, June–July 1666 and because of the matters debated. How vigorous then was the Catholic Church if it could assemble in Dublin so openly?

A detailed report from Archbishop Edmund O'Reilly of Armagh to Rome giving his impressions of his first visitation, probably 1662 is worth quoting. Armagh was the least diminished in clergy he reported but most of the bishops were in exile. Many of the dioceses were in the care of vicars with bishops keeping in touch from the continent. There were about 275 diocesan clergy with a goodly proportion of regular clergy. O'Reilly begged that the exiled bishops return to Ireland and that an effort be made to recruit well trained clergy. A key figure in the Synod of 1666 was O'Reilly who arrived dramatically on the evening of Walsh's three-hour speech. He opposed Walsh strongly and Ormond, on the conclusion of the Synod, had him arrested and he was again exiled. He died in Louvain in 1669.

The Remonstrance Affair formed a post-script to the bitter divisions of the forties. Dr Corish in 'The Origins of Catholic Nationalism' (pp. 60–62) points out that it 'might be described as an attempt to provide a theoretical backing for the Anglo-Irish tradition of loyalty, or, less kindly, as an attempt to rationalize the position adopted for political reasons in 1648. . . . the Remonstrance provided the first public vindication of the nuncio.'

Economic aspects of the Restoration period

Outwardly the Restoration period was one of reconstruction as witnessed by a growing prosperity in the towns and a rise in land valuation in the 1670s. Commercial life was strengthened by the growth of a number of new towns: Charleville, Portarlington, Lanesboro' *et al.* The rise of Dublin as a capital city takes place at this period, helped by the rising port of Liverpool across the Channel. The population increased noticeably and a comparison between the travelogues of Elizabethan visitors to Ireland and the regional descriptions of William Molyneux between 1682 and 1685 show a remarkable progress in the state of the countryside.

To offset these improvements, however, the dominant economic policy of England ran counter to Irish interests. Mercantilism decreed that a country's prosperity depended on increasing exports and decreasing imports, thereby maximising on the country's capital of gold bullion. Consequently England cut down on imports from Ireland, prohibiting Irish exports likely to compete with her own even in foreign markets. Severe restrictions were placed on Irish trade with England and the colonies. Irish wool was prohibited except under licence and the growth of an Irish woollen industry carefully pruned lest underselling 'our subjects here and consequently much decay the trade of clothing in this Our Kingdom, which we must not admit'. (Charles II to Ormond).[4] Even more serious were the Cattle Acts of 1663 and 1666. Cattle formed the most valuable export of Ireland in the early sixties, tens of thousands being sent across the Channel annually for fattening on English pastures. With the exclusion of live cattle by the two Acts, Ireland had lost almost her sole export market in this field by 1666. The price of cattle fell to ten or twelve shillings the following year from forty shillings per head a few years previously. Though it was a staggering blow aimed at the political-minded Irish landowners, it was offset by the vigorous provision and victualling trade which sprang up between Ireland, Europe and the colonies. On a subsistence level Ireland became self-sufficient but the prospect of long-term manufacturing industry was pessimistic in the teeth of mercantilist policy in Europe and England's protective Navigation Laws. The real failure of industrial development in Ireland is to be traced to this period rather than a century later; the wealthiest, most influential and enterprising landowners were absentees.

One other factor of importance to Anglo-Irish relations

in the following century takes its rise in the Restoration period. Ireland had been a source of uncertainty, indeed unreliable revenue, to the monarchs of England. The right of the Irish parliament to vote subsidies to the king became an important political lever for the Irish House of Commons, particularly if the king were in financial difficulties. Henceforth the Irish parliament, summoned irregularly, would exercise bargaining powers to extract political concessions from its monarch. As yet this was a potential weapon capable of being used only when parliament was summoned regularly. Meanwhile the exhausted and despoiled nation of Gaelic and Old English inhabitants felt that anti-monarchical forces in England were to be more feared than the Stuart kings; so it happened that they defended the Stuart monarchy once again in its last great struggle with the English parliament.

9 The Last Dissent

James II and the policy of Tyrconnell

The political history of the last years of Charles II was uneventful. 1681 rather than the death of Charles II four years later marks the transition from the policies of Charles II to those of his brother James, duke of York, an enthusiastic convert to Catholicism since his marriage to Mary of Modena. As early as 1681 in Scotland James as heir-designate to his brother's throne obtained an Act guaranteeing that his hereditary rights would not be jeopardised by his conversion to Catholicism. After 1681 royal policy in Scotland became the special interest of James duke of York. The imposition of the Test Act whereby all office-holders in church and state and all electors and members of parliament were required to swear an oath acknowledging the 1560 Confession of Faith presented serious difficulties to Presbyterians. For them to take such an oath was tantamount to renouncing the Covenant, any meetings or leagues convened for determining matters of church and state, and accepting without reservations royal supremacy. For some time the Test Act did not have immediate repercussions. James possessed the loyalty of the nation as a whole; this was noticeable at his accession. His brother Charles had effectively broken much of the ecclesiastical opposition in Scotland and for some years the political and parliamentary opposition was quiet if watchful.

It was the second parliament of James II in 1686 that manifested the way the tide was running in Scotland. James offered free trade with England to the Scots in exchange for the relief of Roman Catholics and the laws against them. There was strong opposition. Parliament adjourned. James had raised the issue of toleration and had received a clear warning.

In actuality there were only about 2,000 Roman Catholics in Scotland, mostly in the highlands. Almost immediately the king began restricting royal favours to those of the king's own religion. There was a rush of converts from among that perennial group who like to salute the rising sun. The earl of Perth became a convert, and chancellor; his brother, secretary of state. Command of Edinburgh Castle was given to the Catholic duke of Gordon. The Abbey of Holyrood was turned into a Roman Catholic chapel. The Jesuits were allowed to open a school and a Catholic printing press was set up. Free worship was allowed to Catholics in their homes, and also to Quakers by royal proclamation.

James, however, did not extend toleration to Presbyterians whom he regarded as 'those enemies of christianity, the field conventiclers whom we recommend you to root out with all severities of our laws'. By 1687, in a second proclamation, James II granted freedom of worship to all the king's subjects. It acted like a boomerang. Hitherto many secret Presbyterians had acquiesced in the state religion and had attended Protestant services. Now congregations at parish churches dwindled and Presbyterians grew in strength, augmented by refugees from Holland. Presbyterians had again a covenanting appeal with hopes of a Presbyterian restoration.

In Ireland a similar transformation was taking place. The execution of Bishop Oliver Plunket in July 1681 on a trumped-up charge of treason was the peak-point of the hysteria surrounding the Popish Plot. His death solidified Catholic feeling and prepared an atmosphere receptive to Tyrconnell's romanising endeavours later on. Early in

1682 Ormond who had behaved with moderation during the Popish Plot scare was invited to England where he was conferred with the title of duke and was consulted frequently by Charles. Towards the middle of 1684 he was unexpectedly ordered back to Dublin and within three months of his return to the city whose new planning he had so carefully supervised, he was dismissed tactfully but firmly by King Charles. The king intimated to him that Laurence Hyde, earl of Rochester, was to replace him as viceroy. Hyde, brother-in-law to James, would innovate changes in the civil and military government of Ireland which, the king assured Ormond, were absolutely necessary.

Behind this appointment were James and his close confidant, Richard Talbot who was to become in succeeding months James' standard-bearer in all matters concerning the catholicising of Ireland. But whereas James worked to advance the cause of Catholicism in Ireland, Talbot outstripped him in advancing his own interests and those of Ireland. The occasional mild reprimands of James fell unheeded. Ironically then, earlier than in England or Scotland, James moved towards disaster in Ireland.

The accession of James to the throne confirmed the romanising trend of his Irish policy. In April 1685 Richard Talbot was made earl of Tyrconnell and together with Justin McCarthy received important commissions in the Irish army. Other Catholic officers were gradually placed in positions of varying importance in the Irish army and were exempted from the oath of Supremacy. James made it obvious that he regarded Tyrconnell, and not Clarendon whom he had nominated lord lieutenant instead of his brother Rochester, as his confidential adviser on Ireland. Increasingly Tyrconnell came to dominate Irish affairs: 'a man of monstrous vanity as well as pride and furious passions', Clarendon wrote bitterly to his brother.

Tyrconnell disliked Clarendon and after a brief visit to

London returned with a commission to control army matters independently of the viceroy in the summer of 1686. Replacement of Protestant by Catholic soldiers was accomplished rapidly. Dr Simms estimates that by the end of September 1686 there were over 5,000 Catholic privates serving in an army of an estimated 7,500. Catholic officers were advanced more slowly but in 1688 the Irish army was a Catholic one.[1]

In the judiciary appointments Clarendon was not notified of the replacement of three Protestant judges by three Catholic ones. The new judges were Thomas Nugent, member of a still prominent Old English family, Denis Daly and Stephen Rice. Like the Catholic army officers they were not obliged to subscribe to the oath. Catholic changes in the administration kept pace with the army appointments: their admittance to corporations, to seats in the privy council, to the offices of magistrates and sheriffs. Yet as long as the Restoration Settlement remained stable, Clarendon made no demur. Tyrconnell's unconcealed intention to change the Restoration Settlement as champion of the Irish Catholic landowners caused widespread disquiet. He himself had benefited from the Settlement and his newly-acquired zeal for revision of the Settlement amazed and frightened the Protestant property holders. From 1686 onwards a persistent exodus from Ireland took place, mainly among the merchant-officer class.

The restoration of Charles II had accomplished a partial restoration of Irish Catholics to their estates but the total effect of the Acts of Settlement and Explanation, and the Court of Claims were dissatisfaction and insecurity on all fronts. James while still duke of York had been proposing a further statutory re-appraisal of the Restoration Settlement, possibly a restoration of half the settlement land to Catholics if Tyrconnell is to be believed. In fact the 'new' interest by the 1680s was not exclusively Protestant, and the formidable lobby which developed from the preservation of the Settlement in substance was composed of some Catholics as well as Protestants. There was the known extent of James' personal estates in Ireland, spread over sixteen counties which made many doubt his basic sincerity in this matter.

Tyrconnell's promotion as deputy to succeed Clarendon was then a decided jolt when it was announced in January 1687. Evelyn the diarist recorded that 'Lord Tyrconnell gone to succeed the lord lieutenant in Ireland, to the astonishment of all sober men, and to the evident ruin of the protestants in that kingdom'. Almost immediately Tyrconnell pushed ahead with preparations for a parliament. The significance of the *quo warranto* issue of the Jacobite corporations is still a matter of some conjecture among historians. Did James II approve of the revocation of existing charters including that of Dublin, or was Tyrconnell anticipating the king's wishes in remodelling the charters? It appeared to contemporaries that King James was choosing to make an issue of the one factor which could bring down his throne, that of religious toleration, now revealed as the familiar threat of popery. Panic set in. The growing numbers of Irish exiles in England was accompanied by the arrival of Irish troops whom James called to his support in England, a situation which recalled Wentworth's Irish army more than forty years previously. If it were merely a question of religious toleration taking place side by side with civil liberty then the action of the English and Scottish people would indeed appear inexcusable. James, however, in his zeal for Catholicism, showed a harsh intolerance for Presbyterianism which in Ireland and in Scotland caused the same unexpected backlash of resistance.

The Ulster Scots by the reign of James II formed a kind of protestant polity. Throughout the seventeenth century they retained a sense of solidarity and the Synod of Ulster claimed jurisdiction over their actions. According to Petty in his *Political Anatomy of Ireland* published in 1671 the Scots Presbyterians in Ulster numbered 100,000. Schomberg reported that when he landed in County Down the majority of the people were Presbyterians. The reaction, in Ulster, to the Declaration of Indulgence was to hold a public fast. Unlike the Covenanters of Scotland, the Irish Presbyterians believed in their hearts that theirs was not only the right to exist but the right to dominate the country. Dr J. C. Beckett remarks: 'Such a body of men, so placed, were little likely to welcome an indulgence when they thought themselves entitled to an establishment'.[2]

Tyrconnell's policy of placing Roman Catholics in advantageous positions gave the same cause for resentment as it did to their co-covenanters in Scotland. In December 1688 an anonymous letter threatening a general massacre was circulated throughout the country and the arrival of William of Orange in Torbay was hailed with relief by the Ulster Scots. The author of a contemporary account, *Narrative of the Siege of Londonderry*, McKenzie, suggests that the Presbyterian ministers in Ulster were the first to think of sending an address to the Prince of Orange. It is still a matter for argument whether the sending of the address meant a formal renunciation of loyalty to James II.

By the beginning of 1689 events in the three kingdoms had again begun to inter-act as they had done in 1641. Throughout the previous year Scotland had manifested no signs of wanting to dislodge James whose small son born in the middle of 1688 seemed a guarantee of the continuity of the Stuart line. Even when the revolution began in England, Scotland was slow to follow suit. After all the Scots did not know William of Orange but when news reached Scotland of James' flight 23 December 1688 the south-west, that hotbed of covenanting Presbyterianism, rose in rebellion against him. The Scottish army had been summoned into England and there was no force to maintain order. In Edinburgh rioting broke out. The mobs sacked Holyrood and defiantly desecrated the royal tombs of more than a hundred kings.

By January 1689 the Ulster Presbyterians had taken matters into their own hands. Walker, the hero of Derry, states in his *True Account of the Siege of Londonderry* (London 1689), and echoed in other contemporary pamphlets, that 'the lords and gentlemen of the counties of Down, Antrim, Armagh and Monaghan associated together to stand on their defence against the Irish'. It is then understandable that the Irish Presbyterians claimed William and Mary as king and queen immediately and became their most ardent supporters. Unlike the Church of Ireland, Irish Presbyterians were not troubled by theories of divine right or non-resistance. The events in Scotland, the defiant jettisoning of the episcopacy was as alarming to the Established Church in Ireland as it was a cause of celebration to Irish presbyterians.

As yet Tyrconnell held the country for James. The constitutional crisis had not polarised political attitudes in Ireland and for a few weeks Tyrconnell was able to play off the Ulster Protestants and William's emissary, Richard Hamilton, with considerable skill. He kept closely in touch with James in France urging him to request money for payment of troops from Louis XIV. By March 1689 Tyrconnell was in command of the whole country save Ulster and Sligo. Though the commander of the Derry garrisons, Lundy, invited the Ulster Presbyterians to resist, there was no indication that Derry crowded with refugees after the break of Dromore was to become in Beckett's phrase 'the most famous siege in British history'.

Early in March James II arrived in Kinsale with a fleet of twenty-two ships and a distinguished group of Irish and English Jacobites and French officers. Tyrconnell met him at Cork and from there to Dublin, the first English king to visit Ireland for nearly three hundred years was accompanied by the cheers of multitudes to the accompaniment of 'The king enjoys his own again'. A few weeks later James impulsively visited Derry with unfortunate consequences for his cause. According to d'Avaux, the French envoy who accompanied James, the king had originally intended to accompany his troops part of the way as preparations for a parliament were already on foot. However the news of the Jacobite victory at Clady near Lifford which filled Derry with refugees caused James to turn towards Derry. His arrival was precipitate. Negotiations were already progressing favourably with the proviso that the Jacobite army should not advance within four miles of the city. Instead James unknowingly proceeded and was fired upon from the walls. Consternation was matched by defiance and resistance hardened into a desperate resolve to hold the city at all costs.

The Patriot Parliament

The parliament which opened in May 1689 has been the subject of admiration by nineteenth-century nationalist historians like Thomas Davis, and of execration by contemporaries, including Jacobite adherents. The 1689 parliament received its most characteristic title from Charles Gavan Duffy, the 'Patriot Parliament'. The interest aroused by this parliament in nationalist historiography lies in its rejection of the claims of the English parliament to legislate for Ireland, and in its veto on appeals to England from the Irish Courts of King's Bench and Common Pleas. Thomas Davis locates its significance in the continued Whig interpretation which made its convening a matter of constitutional dispute, in the influence it exercised on the immediate parliament that followed it with the penal code, and because it furnished the 1782 parliament with principles and a precedent. The contempt poured on this assembly by Williamite contemporaries forces the student of this period to place any evaluation of it in its definite political context.

The parliament which met in Dublin and consisted of a

House of Lords in which fifty-four peers sat, and a House of Commons of 224 members was the product of unusual circumstances. It was Catholic-dominated; only six Protestants sat in the Commons. Tyrconnell had restored Catholic control of the boroughs by his *quo warranto* procedures, and the way ahead to total Catholic control seemed clear by his proposed appointment of sheriffs and by the summoning of a Catholic parliament. Financial pressures were undoubtedly James' first concern when he summoned parliament, not without fears. In his opening speech the king promised relief to anyone injured by the Acts of Settlement and Explanation but he had little expectation of the vehemence with which the repeal of the act was carried both in nature and scope. The Commons rejected out of hand the Lords' moderate Bill and the amendments sent down later. Even when James threatened to dissolve the parliament, he received the reply that he would have to fight the war on his own resources. The Commons' threat to refuse a subsidy was a genuine one. The Bill of Repeal was given royal assent in late June. James wrote the vigorous preamble in his own writing and incidentally gave the Irish view of the war: the rights of the Irish were based on the peace of 1648, the restoration restored them to loyalty and to properties possessed in 1641. Thomas Davis, while allowing the justice of this restoration of property, points out that the Act contains no provisions for the families of those Adventurers who however culpable when they first took possession of the lands, had now occupied them for thirty to forty years and had time and citizenship in their favour. Maxwell, a Jacobite general, summed up well James' dilemma at this point: 'All his other subjects have deserted him; this is the only body of men that he has now to appear for him; he is in their hands and must please them.'

The Bill of Attainder which followed became the bitter core of controversy in this unusual assembly. It confiscated the estates of over 2,000 named persons and James' power of pardoning these was limited to the following November, a period so short that the majority who resided in England were unaware that they were listed. It was not a sectional attainder list however as maintained by whig historians; Protestant and Catholic names mingled with like penalties pronounced against them. The yardstick for confiscation was not religion but loyalty to King James, and the Act is most properly understood in a general setting of land restoration and tenurial re-definition. Dr J. G. Simms sees the Act as central to the proposed Patriot Parliament, because only among the estates of confiscated Williamites would sufficient land be found to compensate those who had forfeited it by the Act of Repeal.

The parliament honoured the principle of religious toleration for all and decreed that landowners pay tithes to their respective churches. James' subsidy was raised by £5,000 to the total of £20,000. Several minor Acts dealing with navigation and the naturalisation of French subjects were passed. Parliament sat between May and July. Thomas Davis sees its importance as a symbol of national solidarity as did Wolfe Tone. 'It boldly announced our national independence in words which Molyneux shouted on to Swift, and Swift to Lucas, and Lucas to Flood, and Flood and Grattan redoubling the cry, Dungannon church rang and Ireland was again a nation.' The real importance of the 1689 parliament in its political context of the Jacobite-Williamite struggle was the brief emergence of a Catholic ascendancy bent on confiscation. It was a claim that depended on military victory and Anthony Dopping, the Protestant bishop of Meath pointed out that it was the division of the skin of a beast which had not yet been caught. The resolution of the Catholic members to establish their ascendancy emerged clearly from the tone of the legislation, but the result of the war was a Protestant ascendancy. Retribution was swift.

The Williamite confiscation of about 270 Jacobite estates encompassing nearly a million acres was the reply of the Irish Protestants to the 1689 parliament.

Progress of the War

No Irish war has left such an indelible impression on the folk-memory of Ireland as the Williamite War. Gaelic poets, balladeers, set-dances and pipe music record the various peak-points of the war. 'Lilibullero' the song that whistled a king out of three kingdoms, the poems of O'Bruadair and Seamas Dall MacCuarta, Fallaí Luimní and the Bridge of Athlone, (well-known set-dances), the parades commemorative of the Boyne in Belfast and the Apprentice Boys' March in Derry are conscious invocations of a remembered past. It was the most exciting and colourful war of the plantation centuries, the last great stand when two sides were fairly evenly balanced, colonist and native Irish.

It was more. In his study, *Ireland in the European System,* (vol. i, 1920), Dr James Hogan demonstrated the growing links between Ireland and Europe throughout the sixteenth century. The Elizabethan wars, in particular, showed up the pattern of expectations which native Irish sought for when they rejected an English monarch; it was to Spain and France they looked for help, and if victorious, for a future king. Papal intervention was the other European strand that wove itself into the Irish wars of the sixteenth and seventeenth centuries; in the beginning through means of papal letters and bulls, and eventually through the presence of envoys and a nuncio. The Williamite War took the European interest a stage further: for the first time two kings, both claiming the throne of three kingdoms confronted each other at the Battle of the Boyne. This in itself was unusual but even more piquant to a Europe now wide-awake to the drama of the war was the grim duel renewed on Irish soil between William of Orange and Louis XIV for domination of northern Europe in the third great French war of Louis' reign. Jacobite and Williamite mixed with Frenchman and Dutch in a cosmopolitan setting which rang familiarly with Irish place-names. Lieutenant General Maumont was killed before the Derry Walls. The duke of Berwick and Patrick Sarsfield advanced on Enniskillen. Marshal Schomberg landed in Carrickfergus. King William of Orange and King James Stuart met at the Boyne. A Sarsfield defended Limerick and a Frenchman, St Ruth planned the strategies of the battle of Aughrim. It was a splendid roll-call and reverberated throughout Europe. Dr J. G. Simms, the historian of Jacobite Ireland, points out that 'in the Europe of the day (the Boyne) represented a signal success for the Grand Alliance against Louis XIV . . . from the Jacobite point of view Aughrim, with its heavy death-roll, was the decisive battle of the war.'

It was a war in which geographical considerations, chance and skill all played a part. The relief of the siege of Derry was a daring manoeuvre yet the landing of Schomberg proved a damp squib, and prolonged the war with the odds of victory still indecisive. The landing of William of Orange was a mark of prestige – and the debacle of James' forces at the Boyne unfortunate for Irish morale. The taking of Dublin was not the climax of the war because the line of the Shannon with French ships of war, French commanders and troops to man Athlone and Limerick invested Connacht with a military importance never before or after exploited in quite the same manner. The final capitulation of Galway was a fitting end to a war which represented the hopes and ambitions of Irish and Anglo-Irish who took their last stand in the centre of that 'Pale' designed for them by Cromwell.

The Treaty of Limerick

The Treaty of Limerick was the result of complex negotiations. Patrick Sarsfield became the chief negotiator on the

Jacobite side and a Dutchman, Ginkel, acted as William's representative. Tyrconnell died suddenly in August 1691 before the second siege of Limerick began and responsibility for the siege and ultimately for the Settlement, rested upon Sarsfield. It was Sarsfield who took the initiative in the matter of capitulation. With a Scottish Jacobite named Wauchope he came to the Williamite camp asking for a cease-fire on the evening of 23 September 1691. Ginkel immediately sent word to the lords justices to join him in the negotiations but Sarsfield maintained the lead in discussion. He was supported by Dominick Maguire, Catholic Archbishop of Armagh, John Brenan Catholic Archbishop of Cashel, and Sir Toby Butler, solicitor-general for Ireland.

The articles of treaty which emerged from the talks of the next ten days concerned military and civil agreements. The Irish negotiators had little difficulty over the military articles which were tripartite, because of French involvement. They provided for the Irish army's freedom of movement to go to France; transport for the journey would be supplied by Ginkel. The civil articles were the real bone of contention both at the level of negotiation and in their repercussions subsequently. The negotiators were aware that the civil articles would be enforced on the entire Catholic population, including the citizens of the capitulated cities and the members of the Irish army. The Irish negotiators attached the utmost importance to the terms insisting that they should be guaranteed by an Act of parliament. Ginkel's instructions precluded him from offering terms of any great latitude to Irish Catholics and he rejected the demands for full identity, the restoration of estates to all Catholics, liberty of worship and freedom to hold civil and military appointments and to pursue professions.

Instead Ginkel sent to the Irish negotiators twelve propositions and these formed the basis of the civil articles.

The first article concerned the extent of religious toleration that would be allowed for the future in Ireland: Irish Catholics were to have the same privileges in the practice of their religion as they had enjoyed in the reign of Charles II or as were consistent with the laws of Ireland. The second and fifth articles were concerned with safeguarding the persons and property of the inhabitants of Limerick and of 'all those under their (the Irish army's) protection in the four counties named'. This latter phrase became the famous missing clause which was dropped from the signed copy although Ginkel's secretary, George Clarke, included it in the original draft.

The third and fourth articles concerned particular persons not then resident in Ireland. The sixth article decreed that no law-suits should follow acts committed by either side during the war in the general interests of peace. The Williamite signatories pledged William and Mary to ratify the articles of Limerick within eight months and to 'use their utmost endeavours that the same should be ratified and confirmed in parliament'.

The Treaty of Limerick was, by contemporary judgement, a facile document accomplished in haste and without sufficient reflection on the part of the negotiators. Charles O'Kelly, a Galway Jacobite, in his *Destruction of Cyprus* criticised its formulation: 'the articles were not so warily drawn but room was left for captious exceptions; neither was any article made for assuring the true worship.' It pleased neither the Irish Protestants who thought it too generous to the rebels, nor the Irish Catholics who felt they were entitled to the free exercise of their religion and guarantee of restoration of lands. As for King William, temporarily it relieved him of the nuisance of maintaining an army in Ireland, and ultimately through the action of the Irish parliament, 1692–97, from assuming responsibility for its implementation.

10 The Aftermath of a Treaty

The penal laws reviewed

The terms of the Treaty of Limerick were enacted in the prevailing atmosphere of a colonial parliament. It was to be Ireland's unhappy lot after the Williamite War had ended to become the victim of colonial pressures despite her European position, culture and peoples. Even before the Treaty of Limerick was ratified King William restored the traditional institutions of government as they had existed for centuries in Ireland. The convening of a parliament in October 1692 was the resumption of the old order, not an innovation on William's part, but on this occasion the exclusively Protestant character of the Irish parliament was aggressively discriminatory in a colonial sense. The Cromwellian settlement had classified 'Irish' and 'Catholic' as synonymous. The Williamite Settlement as ratified by the Dublin parliament gave the legal fiction a status in law which denied the rights of citizenship to the servile and dispossessed population of the colony.

No consideration of colonialism in seventeenth-century Ireland would be complete without a survey of its most powerful instrument, the penal laws. In the administration of the penal laws two clear phases may be distinguished; the Elizabethan Church Settlement and the enactment of the Penal Code in the 1692–97 parliaments. The Elizabethan Church Settlement was penal in its enactments. The 1560 Acts of the Irish parliament, passed in a questionable manner, were designed to buttress an established state

Church. This was in keeping with the times. Royal supremacy was restored over the Church of Ireland. As a test of loyalty, a new oath of supremacy was imposed on all office-holders, ecclesiastical and lay. The Act of Uniformity of Prayer was a prescription enforceable by justices of the peace and other civil officials. All were obliged to attend the service on Sundays and other days under pain of forfeiture or fine. The election of bishops was abolished, the Crown nominating to vacancies by letters patent.

Dr Edwards has pointed out that one paragraph of the Act of Uniformity was peculiar to Ireland: the substitution of Latin for the English vernacular in the use of the Book of Common Prayer. The excuse proffered was the difficulty of using and reading Irish type, but it is a matter for debate that if the Elizabethan Church Settlement was the strategy of an intensive evangelising action such as the Spaniards accomplished in Spanish South America, then the refusal or inability to come to grips with the problem of communicating the Reform Service to the native population was short-sighted. By the reign of James I the implications were clear: the Established Church was to be a colonial one, and all who had any part in Irish administration were obliged to conform. The playing off of Old English recusant and new English colonist which was so much a feature of this Jacobite period can be interpreted as part of the struggle to dominate the bureaucracy previously established by the Tudors as the method of governing Ireland. In an earlier chapter we have noted the type of office-holder cited in the Acts of Supremacy and Uniformity: everyone from a bishop to a curate, from a judge to the clerk of the court, mayors and members of town corporations, all holders of sinecures, university members whether teachers or graduates, minors-at-law before coming of age and so on. It is not hard to guess that an office-holder was also a member of the gentry, or depending on the importance of the office, a member of the great landed class. If we take a look at the penalties and fines imposed for non-observance it seems obvious that they were aimed at the salaried, monied or landed classes. The penalties for non-observance of the Act of Uniformity were for office-holders, six months in gaol and deprivation of income for twelve months for a first offence. If anyone showed disrespect for the liturgy by word or deed, he was liable to forfeit a hundred marks to the Crown. The penalty for non-observance of the Act of Supremacy was lifelong incapacity to hold office, loss of property and the charge of high treason. Sir John Davies in his tour of Munster was preoccupied with the problem of recusancy and fines. In Dungarvan he narrated the following:[1]

> From Waterford we passed to Cork, and by the way we lodged the first night at Dungarvan where, the next morning being Sunday, we heard a sermon, at which all the people of that poor town were present, one or two of the chief burgesses excepted who desired a time of conference, which was granted unto them. This general conformity was wrought by the presence of the Lord President the week before, when he passed that way from Cork to Waterford. Here, when I perceived how easily the inferior and common sort of people are drawn to the Church, I began to doubt whether it were not a preposterous course to proceed against the wealthier sort of aldermen and citizens first, because they being proved by reason of their wealth, and consequently wilful, and withal most laboured and wrought by the priests as being best able to entertain them, are resolved to suffer at first for the credit of their cause, presuming this storm will quickly be overblown, as it hath been in former times; and so by their example they make the multitude more obstinate.

Sir John Davies goes on to comment that with the common people 'the pain of twelve pence Irish for every Sunday or holiday, which amounts not to three pounds sterling for a whole year' was not worth the trouble but a little later Davies adds significantly that in Limerick merchants were indicted at the rate of 200 marks sterling.

It would seem that the two classes aimed at in the Elizabethan Code were the Old English and the New English: the former to bring them into line, the latter to keep them in allegiance to the Crown policy. Did the central government have the power to enforce these laws? In the reign of Elizabeth they were enforced sporadically, often as acts of retaliation generated in the atmosphere of rebelliousness. The firm rejection of the State Church by the Old English was a complicating factor. Irritation over plantation schemes helped the Old English to identify colonialism and the Anglican Church as two hostile innovations in sixteenth-century Ireland. There was the added feeling that they were being passed over in favour of the New English for government posts. Conversely the response of the central government to its own campaign of penal laws was an inability to enforce them consistently, or even at times to take them seriously.

It is only with the accession of James I that the Acts of Supremacy and Uniformity became a disagreeable reality in the lives of the inhabitants of Ireland. It was during his reign that Ireland came under common law which meant that all office-holders had recourse to the same system of law. The Catholic Counter-Reformation was taking root with a strong appeal and sense of identity both for native Irish and Old English. The fact that the Catholic Church was an outlaw Church, and not an instrument of the government and was without visible means of support was eventually to transform it into a centre of nationalistic impulses. The most striking feature of the reigns of James I and Charles I in the matter of recusancy politics was the complicated and ingenious business of raising the king's revenue. Elizabeth I had left a debt to her successor. The

Nine Years War was costing well over a million pounds sterling a year from 1596 onwards. Ireland to the Tudors was an expensive liability, and much of that expense was paid out of the private purse of the monarch. James I thought differently and it is possible to see in the enforcement of recusancy fines and forfeitures from the reign of James I onwards an elaborate form of taxation. How else explain an all-out effort towards Anglican conformity at a period when a successful colony of Scottish Presbyterians had settled in Ulster. The Ulster Presbyterian colonists were as little attracted to the Episcopalian Church of Ireland as they were to Irish counter-reformation Catholicism. The history of seventeenth-century Presbyterianism was in the main that of a tightly-knit social group determined to maintain their own Church, independent of the established one.

Recusancy continued to be a dominant theme during the reign of Charles I. It was the background to the negotiations of the Graces between King Charles and the Old English. In the interim before Wentworth's arrival Boyle, earl of Cork, advocated strongly the application of recusancy fines as a means of raising revenue. He was thinking in particular of the Old English, but with the arrival of Wentworth and the outbreak of war recusancy ceased to be a dominant political issue.

The Irish parliament

For a brief period the Cromwellian plantation entertained the concept of complete evangelisation but as Goblet points out the new political theories of Harrington's *Oceana*, and Hobbes *Leviathan* profoundly influenced the concept of the plantation as designed by Sir William Petty.[2] Restoration Ireland was not, then, a return to a former set of political groupings. It was clear from the Restoration Parliament that its composition was Protestant in a discriminatory sense, dominated by the Cromwellian interest.

However, the Restoration Settlement and Charles' many pardons cooled the politico-religious tension on which the quest for land was based after Cromwell but gradually Ireland was drawn into the final political drama of the Stuarts and their English subjects. The complete logic of the situation emerged after 1691 with the stabilising of the Williamite Settlement: a dominant landed class that was English-centred whose dependence on English power created the basis for socio-cultural change.

That change was effectively maintained by the enactment of the property-motivated penal laws. Henceforth the old division among Irish Catholics became obsolete as the Catholic gentry were assimilated into one or other of the groupings. The broad achievements of the Restoration-Williamite Settlements resulted in the ruin of the majority of the old land-holders. Those who held on were the great magnates, the Marquis of Antrim, the earl of Clanricard, the earl of Clancarty, the lords of the Pale. In Kerry where there had been 540 Catholic landowners in 1641, there were scarcely any by 1697. In Wexford there had been 152 landowners, now there was not a single one. In Cork MacCarthy Reagh, O'Sullivan Beare, the MacCarthys of Duhallow lost their huge possessions. In Ulster the Magennis of Iveagh lost tenure; in Leinster, Lord Clanmalier was swept away, and in Westmeath the barons of Rathconrath disappeared. In Connacht O'Connor Dhú and O'Conor Sligo were dominated and in general the smaller Irish gentry around Kilkenny, south Tipperary and south Wexford disappeared. Gaelic culture in the first half of the eighteenth century became a peasant culture, popular, oral and Catholic in expression. The Williamite victory gave to the ruling class a century and a half of what Orme calls 'unparalleled development and remodelling at the hands of a favoured minority, the Protestant ascendancy'.[3] Colonisation of Ireland was completed. The Huguenot settlements after the revocation of the Edict of Nantes in 1685 were town-based and the Palatine immigrants of 1709, about 3,000 in number, exerted little influence on the elements of a society kept artificially unassimilated by a ruling class.

Parliament faithfully reflected the distribution of privileges at the end of the seventeenth century, both in its exclusively establishment composition and in the absence of representatives of significant groups. The Irish parliament which met in October 1692 was not prepared to extend legal toleration without a test act to their late Presbyterian allies. Sir Richard Cox who led the opposition against dissenters in the Irish privy council, when dropped by Lord Sidney, William's lord lieutenant, commented: 'the true reason was, because I was a firm churchman, and stopped a bill for "liberty of conscience", by saying I was content every man should have liberty "of going to heaven", but I desired nobody might have liberty of coming into government but those who would conform to it.' Archbishop King later took up a similar position as leader in the House of Lords in the 1695 parliament. The campaign was directed against the Presbyterians of Ulster because they represented a direct threat to the Church party by the strength of their position. Like their Catholic counterparts who had no voice in parliament the Presbyterians of Ulster were a cohesive organised religious group, more a denomination than a sect by reason of their numbers, their system of church government and their religious practices. In the end the Tudor and Stuart centuries in Ireland had produced only a shift in the politics of exclusion and in the methods by which the parliament was made to work.

Yet before the end of that decade a new note was heard. William Molyneux, a member of the House of Commons, in 1698 published a pamphlet, *The case of Ireland's being bound by acts of parliament in England stated,* in which he examined—in relation to the commercial interests of his

The Parliamentary Boroughs at the end of the
seventeenth century

own class—the constitutional strait-jacket which circumscribed the free functioning of the Irish parliament. His book was ordered to be burnt publicly but Molyneux asserted an important truth: legislative independence of the Irish parliament henceforth was related to the uninhibited development of the commercial and economic interests of the country.

Significant, if unnoticed changes had, in fact, taken place by the end of the Stuart century. The basis of local government, so tenuously established throughout the previous century was now broad-based and permanent. Though the bulk of the population was unenfranchised all parts of the country were represented by parliamentary constituencies. One system of law operated and in general was obeyed. Attachment to the monarch, whether in the form of disenchantment as with the Tudors or loyalty as in the case of the Stuarts was no longer a disturbing factor in the maintenance of political peace. The country settled down to a long century of public order which concealed from the rulers the passions and aspirations of the ruled.

Bibliography

POSSIBLY the ideal kind of bibliography for a short volume such as this is one in which general and particular studies are juxtaposed, affording the reader the opportunity to read in depth or acquire another dimension. For a general history of the sixteenth and seventeenth centuries, Bagwell's volumes, *Ireland under the Tudors* (reprinted 1963), and *Ireland under the Stuarts (idem)* are still invaluable, supplemented by J. C. Beckett, *A short history of Ireland* (1952 and subsequent editions), and for seventeenth-century Ireland, *The Making of Modern Ireland, 1603–1923,* (1966). For the English Tudor background, S. T. Bindoff, *Tudor England* (Penguin 1950) and G. W. O. Woodward, *Reformation and resurgence, 1488–1603* (1963) are still the most satisfactory in their treatment of Ireland, though G. R. Elton, *England under the Tudors* (1955) influenced the first chapters of this study. A. L. Rowse is stimulating but erratic on Irish affairs in his *Expansion of Elizabethan England* (1955) and J. E. Neale excellent when he touches on the Irish parliament in his two-volume, *Elizabeth I and her Parliaments* (1955). C. Falls, *Elizabeth's Irish Wars* (1958) is valuable but should be read in conjunction with G. A. Hayes-McCoy, *Scots mercenary forces in Ireland, 1565–1603* (1939).

For the seventeenth century G. Aylmer, *The Struggle for the Constitution 1603–1689. England in the Seventeenth Century* (1963) is to be recommended; Gordon Donaldson, *Scotland, James V to James VII* (1965) has a few valuable insights on Irish affairs but in the opinion of the writer S. R. Gardiner is still unsurpassed when dealing with Irish affairs from an English standpoint in his *History of England* and *History of the Great Civil War* (1886–93).

For the earlier sections of this volume Philip Wilson, *The Beginnings of Modern Ireland* (1912); C. L. Falkiner, *Illustrations of Irish history* (1904); R. D. Edwards, *Church and State in Tudor Ireland* (1935) are important and the articles by D. B. Quinn, 'Henry VIII and Ireland, 1509–34' in *Irish Historical Studies* vol xii, and 'Government printing and the publication of the Irish statutes in the sixteenth century' in *R.I.A. Proc.* 14, sect. C., are essential reading for a deeper exploration of English policy in Ireland. No full-scale study of the Reformation has appeared in the last thirty years and the studies by Canice Mooney 'The first impact of the Reformation' and F. M. Jones 'The counter-reformation' in *History of Irish Catholicism* ed. P. J. Corish (1967 and subsequently) afford tantalising glimpses, rather than a rounded analysis of sixteenth-century Irish ecclesiastical history. However R. D. Edwards 'Ireland, Elizabeth I and the Counter-Reformation' in *Elizabethan Government and Society* ed. S. T. Bindoff *et al.* (1961) merits close study.

Turning to the topic of colonisation, W. F. T. Butler's two classics, *Confiscations in Irish history* (1918) and *Gleanings from Irish history* (1925) are central to any study of the plantations. D. B. Quinn has added greatly to our understanding of Irish colonial theory and practice by his articles and books, the following in particular were used as background material for this volume: *The Elizabethans and the Irish* (1966); *Raleigh and the British Empire* (1943); 'Ireland in sixteenth century European expansion' in *Historical Studies I* (1958); 'The Munster plantation, problems and opportunities' in *Cork Hist. Soc. Journal* 71 (1966); 'Sir Thomas Smith (1513–77) and the beginnings of English colonial policy' in *Amer. Phil. Soc. Proc.*, 89; 'A discourse of Ireland 1599' in *R.I.A. Proc.* 47 sect. c. In different ways, J. Hogan, 'The Triucha Cét and related land measurements' in *R.I.A. Proc.* 38 sect. c; E. McCracken, *The Irish Woods since Tudor times* (1971); T. W. Moody, *The Londonderry Plantation, 1609–41* (1939) and G. A. Hayes-McCoy, *Ulster and other Maps* (1964) add other perspectives to a study of land and countryside in these centuries. Seventeenth-century Ireland has summoned some of their best work from a group of distinguished historians: H. Kearney, *Strafford in Ireland 1633–41* (1959); A. Clarke, *The Old English in Ireland, 1625–42* (1966); E. Strauss, *Sir William Petty* (1954); E. Mac Lysaght, *Irish life in the seventeenth century* (1939); J. G. Simms, *The Williamite Confiscation in Ireland, 1690–1703* (1956); C. Petrie, *The Jacobite Movement* (1948); J. C. Beckett, *Protestant dissent in Ireland, 1687–1780* (1948).

The variety of specialised studies of seventeenth-century Irish history bears testimony to the significance of this century in the estimation of historians, cf. 'Thirty years' work in Irish history' in *Irish Historical Studies,* XV, No. 60 and XVI, No. 61. However, scholarship is heaviest in well-worked areas: political history, history of the Catholic Church, history of the Irish language and literature, and military history. The century is noticeably thin on the history of agriculture, business and financial history, and geographical history. Social and economic history, including the history of architecture has produced a number of highly informative studies but little analysis. The history of administration still awaits its historian, so also does the history of culture. At the risk of appearing idiosyncratic the author recommends the following short-list to the reader as offering fresh insights and new explorations. H. Kearney, 'Mercantilism in Ireland 1620–40' in *Historical Studies I* (1958); T. Ranger, 'Strafford in Ireland: a revaluation' in *Past and Present,* 19 (1961); D. F. Cregan, 'Some members of the Confederation of Kilkenny' in

Measgra i gCuimhne Mhicíl Uí Chléirigh (1944); J. Bossy, 'The Counter-Reformation and the People of Catholic Ireland, 1596–1641' in *Historical Studies 8* (1971); R. A. Butlin, 'Urban genesis in Ireland, 1556–1641' in *Liverpool Essays in Geography*, ed. R. W. Steel and R. Lawton (1967); S. O'Tuama, Téamaí iasachta i bhfilíocht pholaítiúil na Gaeilge 1600–1800' in *Éigse XI* (1965); K. Bottigheimer, 'English money and Irish land: the "Adventurers" in the Cromwellian Settlement of Ireland' in *Journal of British Studies*, VII, No. 1 (1967); T. J. Kiernan: *The financial administration of Ireland* (1930); F. R. Bolton, *The Caroline tradition of the Church of Ireland with particular reference to Bishop Jeremy Taylor* (1958); K. T. Hoppen, 'The Royal Society and Ireland' in *Royal Society of London, Notes and Records*, 18 (1963); 20 (1965).

Published documentary sources for the Tudor and Stuart centuries are a valuable background to an understanding of the period. The following highly selective list will introduce the reader to the charm of original sources: M. Brady, ed., *State Papers concerning the Irish Church; State Papers Henry VIII*, vols II & III; *Calendar State Papers Ireland 1603–1625; Calendar Carew Manuscripts*, 6 volumes; *The Chronicle of Ireland*, Irish Manuscript Commission 1933; *The Walsingham Letter Book*, ditto 1959; *Letters and Papers relating to the Irish rebellion*, 1642–46, IMC 1936; *The Civil Survey 1654–56* IMC 1931–61; 'Ulster Plantation Papers' in *Analecta Hibernica* 8 (1938); Sir John Davies, *Discovery of True Causes: why Ireland was never truly conquered* (1970); L. O'Cléirigh, *The Life of Aodh Ruadh O Domhnaill* 2 volumes (1948–57); W. Knowler, ed., *The earl of Strafford's letters and dispatches*, 2 volumes (1739); W. Penn, *My Irish Journal, 1669–70*, ed. J. Grubb (1952); *Calendar of State Papers, domestic series Charles II*, vols 26–28; *James II* vols 1–3 (for interesting Irish material).

References

Chapter 2

[1]The Reformation Parliament of 1536–37 has been the subject of two recent studies: R. D. Edwards, 'The Irish Reformation Parliament of Henry VIII, 1536–7' in *Historical Studies VI* ed. T. W. Moody, London 1968, B. Bradshaw, 'The opposition to the ecclesiastical legislation in the Irish reform parliament' in *Irish Historical Studies, XVI* (1969). The author is grateful to B. Bradshaw for bringing to her notice the precise effect of the fall of Cromwell on Archbishop Browne's career, cf. B. Bradshaw, 'George Browne, First Reformation Archbishop of Dublin, 1536–1554' in *Journal Eccles. History*, 21 (1970).

[2]*State Papers Henry VIII*, II, 297.

[3]P. Wilson, *The Beginnings of Modern Ireland*, Dublin and London 1912.

[4]Archdall, *Monasticon Hibernicum*, II, 292–5.

Chapter 3

[1]W. F. T. Butler, *Confiscations in Irish History*, 10–11, draws attention to the significance of the Act of Absentees.

[2]*S. P. Hen. VIII*, III, 332.

[3]*Calendar of State Papers Ireland (1509–1573)*.

[4]W. F. T. Butler, *Gleanings from Irish History*, 1925 expands somewhat his article 'The policy of Surrender and Regrant' in *Journal Royal Soc. Antiq. Ireland* 43 (1913).

[5]D. B. Quinn, 'Ireland and Sixteenth Century Expansion' *Historical Studies I*, ed. T. D. Williams, London 1958.

Chapter 4

[1]P. Wilson, 'Writings of Sir James Ware and Forgeries of Robert Ware' in *Transactions Bibliographical Society*, 15 (1917).

[2]R. D. Edwards, *Church and State in Tudor Ireland*, Dublin 1935, 181.

[3]D. B. Quinn, 'Government printing and the publication of the Irish statutes in the sixteenth century' in *Proceedings Royal Irish Academy*, 49 (1943) sect. C2.

[4]M. J. Bonn, *Die englische Kolonisation in Irland* 1906.

[5]G. A. Hayes-McCoy, 'Strategy and tactics in Irish Warfare, 1595–1601' in *I.H.S.* 2 (1941).

Chapter 5

[1]R. D. Edwards, *Church and State in Tudor Ireland* Dublin 1936, 68.

[2]N. B. White, *Extents of Irish Monastic Possession 1540–41,* 1943. The pattern of dissolution may be traced 1539–40 in *Extents:* Dublin 12, Carlow 6, Cork 20, Kildare 18, Kilkenny 14, Tipperary 19, Waterford 7, Wexford 12.

[3]Archdall, *Monasticon Hibernicum,* I, (1873), 236.

[4]*Cal. Fiants Henry VIII,* 325.

[5]E. McCracken, 'The Woodlands of Ireland circa 1600' in *I.H.S.* XI, (1959) 271.

[6]Consult S. MacGiollarnaith, *Annála Beaga,* 1941; *Civil Survey* ed. Simington, for folk tradition (1931–61).

[7]C. L. Falkiner, 'The Woods of Ireland' in *Illustrations of Irish History,* 1904; *Cal. S. P. Ire., 1606–08,* 211.

[8]D. B. Quinn, 'Edward Walsh's "Conjectures" concerning the state of Ireland (1552)' in I.H.S. V, 303–22; 'Sir Thomas Smith (1513–77) and the beginnings of English colonial policy' in *American Phil. Soc. Proc.,* 89 (1945); 'The Munster Plantation: Problems and Opportunities' in *Cork Historical and Archaeological Society Journal,* 71 (1966); 'Ireland in Sixteenth Century European expansion' in *I.H.S.* 1, (1958); 'A Discourse of Ireland c.1599' ed. Quinn, in *R. I. A. Proc.,* 47 sect. C.

[9]A. L. Rowse, *Sir Richard Grenville of the 'Revenge',* 1937; D. B. Quinn *Raleigh and the British Empire,* 1943.

[10]Quinn, 'Sir Thomas Smith (1513–1577) and the beginnings of English colonial theory', *loc. cit.,* 543–60.

[11]C. L. Falkiner 'The Counties of Ireland: their origin, constitution, and gradual delimitation' in *Illustrations of Irish History,* 1904, 103–42.

[12]J. Davies, *Discovery of the True Causes why Ireland was never subdued,* 1939.

[13]J. T. Gilbert (ed.), *Aphorismical Discovery* 1, 1879, 325.

[14]Consult P. Power, *Crichad an Chaoilli,* 1932, 1–32; also Begley's discussion of the Munster Plantation in *Diocese of Limerick,* 1927, 1, 129ff.

[15]J. Hogan, 'The Triucha Cet and related land measurements' in *R. I. A. Proc.,* 38 (1943) sect. C7.

[16]In addition to Hayes-McCoy, *Ulster and Other Maps,* 1964; and M. C. Andrews, *The Map of Ireland 1300–1700,* 1924 and *Ireland in Maps,* 1901, the following articles are useful: R. Dunlop 'Sixteenth

century maps of Ireland' in *English Hist. Review*, 20 (1905) and J. J. Westropp 'Early Italian maps of Ireland' in *R. I. A. Proc.*, 30 (1912–13) sect. C, 361ff.

[17]Deputy Perrot in *The Chronicle of Ireland*, ed. Wood; cf. Jobson Map, Plate I in Hayes-McCoy, *Ulster and Other Maps*.

[18]*Ulster and Other Maps*, xii. *Cal. S. P. Ire. Hen. VIII*, 117.

[19]J. Buckley ed. 'The battle of Liscarroll 1642' from a tract in British Museum in *Journal Cork Hist. and Archaeol. Soc.*, Series 2, vol. 4 (1898).

[20]*Journal of the house of commons of the kingdom of Ireland*, i (1778) 42.

[21]*Cal. S. P., Ire.*, 1591–2, 469.

[22]The Desmond Survey is in process of being edited by Professor John Murphy, University College, Cork, but cf. Butler, *Confiscations*, 35.

[23]D. B. Quinn, 'The Munster Plantation: Problems and Opportunities', *loc. cit.*, 19–40.

[24]H. G. Leask, 'Early Seventeenth Century Houses in Ireland' in *Studies in Building History*, ed. E. M. Jope, 1961, 243–56; M. P. Waterman, 'Some Irish Seventeenth Century Houses and their Architectural Ancestry', *loc. cit.*, 251–75.

[25]Landsdowne MS 78, f. 32 in British Museum, cf. Quinn, 'Munster Plantation: Problems and Opportunities' 26, note.

[26]Eochy O'Hussey's 'Ode to Hugh Maguire', E. tr. Frank O'Connor in *A Book of Ireland* London 1959, 85.

[27]See especially Sir John Davies' account of Munster and Ulster 1606 in *Cal. S. P. Ire., 1606–08*, 463ff.

[28]T. W. Moody, *The Londonderry Plantation, 1609–1641*, 1939.

[29]See notes by V. Treadwell in *Ulster Journal Archaeology* 23 (1960–) 126–37; E. M. Jope 'Scottish style castles in the North of Ireland', *loc. cit.*, 14 (1951).

[30]Davies' comments are in *Cal. S. P. Ire., 1606–08*, 463ff.

[31]E. Estyn Evans, *Irish Folkways* London 1957, 44, 50, 59, 102. Also V. B. Proudfoot, 'Rural Settlement in Ireland' in *Advancement of Science* (15) 1959, 336–8.

[32]D. B. Quinn, *The Elizabethans and the Irish*, U.S.A. 1966.

[33]For a succinct account of the growth of towns in this period cf A. R. Orme, 'The World's Landscapes', in *4 Ireland* ed. J. M. Houston, 115–129; also G. Gamblin, *The Town in Ulster* 1951.

Chapter 6

[1]H. Hammerstein has demonstrated the importance of education in her study 'Aspects of the Continental Education of Irish Students in the reign of Queen Elizabeth I' in *Historical Studies VIII*, ed. T. D. Williams, Dublin 1971; Dr P. J. Corish in 'The Origins of Catholic Nationalism',

vol. 3. in *History of Irish Catholicism* traces the fusion between the forces of Irish nationalism and the Catholic religion in seventeenth-century Ireland.

[2]H. R. McAdoo, *John Bramhall and Anglicanism*, Dublin 1964, 9, and R. Buick Knox, *James Ussher Archbishop of Armagh*, Cardiff 1967, 16–23.

[3]R. D. Edwards, 'Ireland, Elizabeth I and the Counter-Reformation' in *Elizabethan Government and Society*, Essays presented to Sir John Neale 1961, 315–39.

[4]A. Clarke, *The Old English in Ireland*, 1625–42, London 1966, 15–27.

[5]See discussion of the Graces in Clarke, *op. cit.*, 28–59.

[6]The author is indebted to Fr Conor Ryan for ideas appearing here and in the following paragraphs from an unpublished thesis 'The Emergence of Royal Absolutism in Ireland' presented to the Faculty of Philosophy, Maynooth University College (1970).

[7]A. Clarke, 'Ireland and the General Crisis' in *Past and Present*. 48 (1970).

Chapter 7

[1]K. Bottigheimer, 'Civil War in Ireland: The Reality in Munster'. in *Emory University Quarterly* (1966).

[2]W. D. Love, 'Civil War in Ireland: Appearances in Three Centuries of Historical Writing' in *Emory University Quarterly* (1966).

[3]J. C. Beckett, 'Confederation of Kilkenny' in *Historical Studies* 2 (1959); P. Corish, 'Ireland's first papal nuncio' in *Irish Ecclesiastical Record*, 81 (1954); J. Lowe, 'Charles I and the Confederation of Kilkenny' in *I.H.S.* 14 (1964); T. L. Coonan, *The Irish Catholic Confederation and the Puritan Revolution* (1954) but see Beckett review in *I.H.S.* XI, (1958).

[4]T. Carlyle, *Cromwell's Letters and Speeches*, II, 98–110.

[5]Bonn, *Die englische Kolonisation in Ireland* 1906.

Chapter 8

[1]G. M. Goblet, *La Transformation de la Geographie Politique de l'Irlande au XVIIe Siècle* I Paris 1930, 53.

In the section entitled 'Origins of the Cromwellian Settlement', Goblet outlines the development of colonial thought in England, dwelling on Harrington's *L'Oceana* 1656.

[2]A. R. Orme, 'The World's Landscapes', *4 Ireland* ed. J. M. Houston, 129.

[4]*Cal. S. P. Ire., 1666–9, 714*.

Chapter 9.
[1]J. G. Simms, *Jacobite Ireland*, 1685–91, 25.
[2]J. C. Beckett, *The Presbyterian Dissent*, 13–39.

Chapter 10
[1]*Cal. S. P. Ire.*, *1604–16*, 466.
[2]Goblet, 'l'Irlande-colonie' 52–91 in *La Transformation de la Geographie Politique de l'Irlande au XVIIe Siècle I*, Paris 1930.
[3]A. R. Orme, *op. cit.*, 130.

Index

207

ACKNOWLEDGMENTS

Grateful acknowledgment is made to the following for permission to reproduce maps and photographs in this book:

Dr. J.K. St Joseph, Director in Aerial Photography, University of Cambridge; Commissioners of Public Works in Ireland; J.C. Beckett and Faber and Faber; A.R. Orme and Longmans; Prof. G. Hayes-McCoy; Finnuala O'Connell.